DOWN THE UP STAIRCASE

DOWN THE UP STAIRCASE

Three Generations of a Harlem Family

BRUCE D. HAYNES and SYMA SOLOVITCH

 COLUMBIA UNIVERSITY PRESS   New York

Columbia University Press gratefully acknowledges the generous support for this book provided by Publisher's Circle Chair Anya Schiffrin.

Columbia University Press
Publishers Since 1893
New York   Chichester, West Sussex
cup.columbia.edu
Copyright © 2017 Columbia University Press
All rights reserved

ISBN 978-0-231-18102-0 (cloth : alk. paper) |
ISBN 978-0-231-54341-5 (e-book)

Cataloging-in-Publication Data is on file at the Library of Congress.

Columbia University Press books are printed on permanent and durable acid-free paper.
Printed in the United States of America

Cover design: Julia Kushnirsky

Cover photograph: Courtesy of Bruce Haynes

To George III

It was spacious, and I dare say had once been handsome, but every discernible thing in it was covered with dust and mould, and dropping to pieces. The most prominent object was a long table with a table-cloth spread on it, as if a feast had been in preparation when the house and the clocks all stopped together.

—Charles Dickens, *Great Expectations*

CONTENTS

ACKNOWLEDGMENTS

THIS work evolved over many years, and many hands have molded it. Matthew Carnicelli was the first to recognize that our story had market potential, while Richard Scheinin, Diana Jean Schemo, and Sara Solovitch—all writers whom we greatly admire—nurtured our literary ambitions and gave us tools to transform them into reality.

The wide scope and varied themes tackled in this book called for critical review and feedback, and we acknowledge the collective efforts of several scholars. Sasha Abramsky brought a journalist's instincts and a wealth of knowledge about poverty, criminal justice, and social welfare policy, while Bill McCarthy offered his keen sociological eye and expertise on incarceration, crime, and juvenile delinquency. George Lipsitz's extraordinary grasp of urban culture, social movements, and African-American history elevated our work considerably. Ralph Richard Banks pushed us to rethink our framing of several key debates and avoid recreating easy tropes about race in America. He also pushed us hard to give more love to some characters and less of a free ride to others. Sharon Zukin recognized early on the merits of conducting an autoethnographic work on life in Harlem. We also thank Prudence Carter, Kai Erikson, Lance Freeman, Aldon

Morris, and Stephen Steinberg, who helped us to refine our arguments and balance the personal, political, and sociological dimensions of the narrative.

Many close friends, including Linda and Stu Bresnick, Jennifer Eberhardt, Rebecca Stein-Wexler, and Tony Wexler, cheered us on from the very start. Some read very raw and early drafts and told us everything we wanted, and desperately needed, to hear. Andy Beveridge offered unwavering enthusiasm and faith in the project.

We are grateful to the outstanding team at Columbia University Press. Editorial Director Eric Schwartz has been an ardent champion for the book, while Todd Manza has conducted painstakingly detailed editing and fact checking.

Certain individuals deserve a category of their own.

One of these is Sara Solovitch, whom we have always depended on for honesty and who delivered—asking tough questions and questioning easy answers. In the final stages, she poured countless hours into editing our manuscript, "killing our darlings," and pushing for deeper, harder truths. She was as caring as she was uncompromising in her standards.

And much of this story could not have been told without the testimony of George Haynes III, who shared painful memories and trusted us to do justice to them. We hope we have not disappointed.

PREFACE

N November 1995, my parents hired a chauffeur and limousine to take them from Sugar Hill, Harlem, to the quaint seashore town of Milford, Connecticut, where my future had finally begun. I had defended my doctoral dissertation that May, married in July, and moved to Connecticut in September to begin teaching at Yale. The limo ride was a once-in-a-lifetime event for my dad, a man who counted kilowatts in pennies and stashed slivers of soap—to be used later for bubble bath. But he was old and frail now, and in a final nod to my mother as well as to his own mortality, he spared no expense for this Thanksgiving Day.

We had long since stopped celebrating holidays at our family home, which had no running water on the main floor. By 1995, my parents were living like squatters in their own house. The pipes were frozen and busted, the roof was beyond repair, and despite the size of the house—nearly five thousand square feet—space was at a premium. Nothing had been dusted, cleared, discarded, or repaired in more than two decades. What was once a formal parlor that hosted W. E. B. Du Bois and other Talented Tenth elites now held the remnants of my brother George's failed business ventures. Half-empty cans of spray paint, battered furniture, and broken appliances heaped on top of one another. . . .

One might have taken the scene for the final stages of a family move—all stacked up and ready to go—except that there was a frozenness about it, a sense of havoc in suspension.

My parents had money and could easily have fixed the place, if they'd so chosen. Pop was collecting a modest monthly pension from the New York State Division of Parole and was sitting on some sweet blue chip stocks he'd bought on margin back in the 1970s. Mom was still employed, as director of quality assurance at the Washington Heights/West Inwood Community Mental Health Center. But, caught in a whorl of reprisal and censure, my parents had let the house fall to ruin until they were living in near-squalor.

That Thanksgiving morning, my mother would have sponge-bathed with Poland Spring water before unwrapping her silk blouse and Dior suit from their plastic encasements, taking care to keep them from brushing against the dust-thick armoire. She would have fixed her makeup in a dirty cracked mirror in a lightless room before carving a path through the stacks of old newspapers and empty water bottles that littered the floor. My father and her mink coat would be waiting for her on the first floor landing. After locking the double doors—a barricade of latches, padlocks, and deadbolts—my parents would have climbed into the back of the sleek limousine and instructed the driver to circle around to pick up my brother George, who was now living in a halfway house just a few blocks away. Then, up Riverside Drive and the Henry Hudson Parkway and on to the world that my mother had always imagined for me.

They arrived in full fanfare. My mother's arms were laden with the customary bags from Zabar's, Citarella's, and Greenberg's Bakery; George followed dutifully with what seemed like a year's supply of toilet paper and paper towels. Pop, haggard and unsteady, carried a long rectangular frame. In it was an oil painting of my grandfather, George Edmund Haynes. On its upper right corner was the signature of Laura Wheeler Waring, a prominent Negro portraitist of the Harlem Renaissance. As I came to learn later, the painting was one of twenty-three *Portraits of Outstanding Americans of Negro Origin* that had appeared at the Smithsonian Institution in 1944 and that toured the country between 1944 and 1946. In the 1960s, most of the portraits were donated to the National Portrait Gallery at the Smithsonian museum, where they remain to this day. The portrait of George Haynes, long buried in our attic, was one of the few that had gone missing.

The painting brought up so many questions. How did Pop come to own it? Why had he never spoken of it? Why was it consigned to the attic? There would never be enough time to get the answers to these questions. Pop died within a month of the visit.

The discovery of the portrait renewed my feelings of ancestral pride but also dredged up memories of pain and dysfunction in my family's history: my dad's conflicted feelings toward his own father, his betrayal of my mother, the ruthless neglect of our home, the murder of one son, the addiction and mental illness of another, the countless wounds and indignities and heartbreaks that my parents had endured. And it underscored the tenuous nature of existence for black, middle-class families like my own. How much protection did the gains of my forefathers, the safety net of a stable two-parent household, and the advantages of expensive private schools ultimately give my brothers and me against becoming three more black male statistics?

In 1967, the sociologists Peter Blau and Otis Duncan conducted their now classic study examining the relationship between parental background and children's occupational outcomes. They found that, among white families, a parent's education and class status were strong predictors of their children's occupational attainment. In black families, however, the children were more likely to end up in the lower strata of the economy regardless of their parents' backgrounds. In many ways, my family defied the odds. All four great-grandparents on my father's side owned land in the South as early as 1880. My grandfather was the first black social economist in the country; his wife, Elizabeth Ross Haynes, was an important children's author of the Harlem Renaissance and an esteemed social scientist of the day. And while my mother's side did not come from money, three successive generations of women in her family were college-educated.

My parents had master's degrees and were gainfully employed. My brothers and I had all attended elite private schools, and I had just completed my PhD and was teaching at Yale University. We owned a three-story brownstone in Harlem, the kind built for a rising moneyed class. Now it stood as a testament to our family's rise and demise over the century. Its walls echoed the voices of three generations of a black middle-class family: the hard-won glories of my grandfather, the whispered regrets and concessions of my parents, the fall from grace of their firstborn, and the wrenching blow that came with the death of their second.

Yet, as our home and family tumbled, my mother held her head high and showed the world a triumphant Negro who wore her wealth and success on her sleeve. She wore designer suits and dazzling diamonds and kept a standing Saturday appointment at Saks Fifth Avenue to get her fingernails and toenails polished—classic red. No one, not even her closest friends, would know that she hauled jugs of water up the stairs each night to sponge-bathe, cook, and flush the toilet. Unable to receive guests in her own house, she entertained in trendy restaurants, often throwing lavish dinner parties for up to thirty people at Empire Szechuan on the Upper West Side. To see her, this dark-skinned beauty with her flawless skin, well into her seventies, snapping her fingers at waiters, ordering General Tso's (which she pronounced "Jen-ĭ-TŌ") chicken like she owned the place, no one would guess what she came home to. Nor would they have been allowed in if they'd asked. It was rare that anyone—neither my mother's friends nor my own, not my wife's family, not even the New York City Fire Department (much to their frustration)— would make their way past the double glass doors of 411 Convent Avenue.

DOWN THE UP STAIRCASE

1

MAD MONEY

THE land on which our house was built (today Convent Avenue between 147th and 148th Streets) was once the most coveted in Manhattan. Just five blocks south stood the original twelve-room country estate of Alexander Hamilton. (The building has been moved twice since that time.) Less than half a block north from our house was Pinehurst mansion—the crown of a hundred-and-ten-acre estate with views of Manhattan Island, the Bronx, New Jersey, and Long Island. The property had been owned by the Bradhursts—one of the oldest colonial families in New York State—since at least the mid-1700s and would remain in that family's hands through the 1860s, when the era of the grand estates of Harlem Heights came to an end.

By the early twentieth century, improvements in urban mass transit led to mass speculation uptown. Architects designed dozens of French provincial, Gothic, Italianate, and Classical Revival houses in Harlem Heights with a view to attracting well-to-do urbanites, who could now commute to their downtown offices. Our own house was built in 1901, at the height of the building frenzy, by the noted New York architect Henri Fouchaux. It was the first of five limestone Revival row houses on the block. The entire row remains framed by a three-foot-high limestone wall and is distinguished by its oriel windows, classical ornaments, and architectural cohesion. The houses are expansive, three stories tall, and include separate garden apartments, originally intended for servants. Most of the first homeowners in the Heights had live-in servants—often young women who had recently immigrated from Ireland, Germany, or Sweden. In some instances, they were blacks who had recently migrated from Virginia and Maryland. The Heights would remain predominantly white until the 1930s, when my grandparents purchased their home at 411 Convent Avenue.

By the time I came along, in 1960, the original sprawl and splendor of the home had been pared back considerably. At nearly five thousand square feet, it was an outrageous space by New York standards, yet our living quarters were confined to two large rooms on the second floor. Back in the early 1950s, my parents had converted the first and third floors into rental units to supplement their social worker incomes. Now, only my mother's friend Dolly—a bubbly light-skinned Guyanese woman—remained. Dolly belonged to a world in which women were neither wives nor mothers but independent beings who frequented the theater and socialized with artists and intellectuals downtown. She was elegant and sophisticated, yet her very presence in our home made us less so. The first floor—with its grand parlor, music room, and formal dining room—was now reduced to an extravagantly appointed urban flat.

The entire second floor was originally designed as a sweeping master bedroom with two spacious rooms—bedroom and sitting area—at opposite ends, cordoned off by sliding pocket doors. Connecting the two rooms was an arched dressing area of dark red oak with built-in his-and-hers mirrored closets and a six-foot-wide marble washbasin encased in wood and flanked by beveled glass medicine cabinets. My parents had transformed this grand space into something much more modest. The water to the basin had been shut off, and the pipes were concealed by a Japanese tapestry tacked to the edge of the vanity. The front room now doubled as a formal living room and our parents' bedroom. Each night the mahogany coffee table with its intricate leather inlay was lifted to the center of the room (its delicate lion paws repositioned on castor cups to protect the massive Oriental carpet from indentation), the tea-green Castro converted to full-size bed, and the eight-foot-high pocket doors slid shut. The Fox police lock—a four-foot-long metal rod that was bolted to the back of the door and affixed diagonally to a brace in the floor—barricaded us in from the stairwell we shared with Dolly.

Despite our cramped quarters, the home was clean and orderly and filled with all the markers of bourgeois respectability. Alongside the double bay window rested a candy-striped satin couch—a pretty but unyielding heirloom that no one sat on. Above it hung a large oil painting of a timeless pastoral scene. The two oval ends of our cherry dining room table remained in drop-down position, diminishing the piece to a small corner table pushed flat against the wall. It was adorned with a teak fruit bowl, whose giant wax apples, oranges, and bananas were individually dusted each week by our housekeeper, Mrs. Cora Grandberry. Just opposite the couch was a marble fireplace filled with faux wood blocks and crowned with a heavy lead mirror.

In the far corner of the room was Pop's "office"—a hefty wooden desk. As a child, I was enchanted by the knickknacks that covered it: a pewter ashtray in the shape of an Indian-head nickel, a chipped clay Buddha bear Pop had made in grade school, a paperweight that magnified print, novelty float pens with mermaids and ships that tossed about, and a full-size ink blotter from the days of quill pens, which, to Pop, signified a well-appointed office. I spent hours marveling over these little treasures, clasping each one and pondering its significance. Eventually I would tire of this ritual and pry into the desk's interiors—fodder for my game of Office. The game consisted of organizing important papers (clipping blank pages together) and making appointments with important people. My mother, who indulged most of my whims and had a real office at Harlem Hospital, pilfered writing pads, pencils, paper clips, rulers, and even a Scotch tape dispenser for me. Eventually Office morphed into Motorcycle Cop, where I posted "road signs" all around the house (little one-inch stickers that Pop had a hard time removing) and handed out speeding tickets to anyone who crossed my path.

My brothers and I slept in the back room, cramped with two twin guest beds, a puffy green armchair, a hulking television console, my parents' dressers, the card table where we ate our meals (when it wasn't being used for our parents' bridge soirees), my brothers' bunk beds, and my crib. White and wooden with bars that dropped just low enough for an adult to reach in, this old-style crib was never intended for toddler transitioning. Yet, with little space for another bed, I stayed in my crib long past the time I could climb out on my own. The possibility of moving into one of the two guest beds had never come up, even though the only guest we ever had—my mother's aunt Corlease from North Carolina—rarely visited and always came alone. It wasn't until I started first grade and my brother George had moved out of the house that I was able to take over the bottom bunk. By then I was already playing poker with my mother and sipping apricot sours with her at social gatherings.

Separate children's quarters had been built on the third floor. Sun poured through the two wide skylights, fading the high Victorian luster of the mahogany banisters. There were two nurseries on the floor, and each had French doors leading to a separate, smaller room intended for nannies. A kitchen—originally the master kitchen from which servants sent food down to the first floor via the dumbwaiter—linked the nurseries together. Though defunct by the sixties, it was the only room in the house that had been truly designed as a kitchen, with built-in cabinets and expansive walls for storage space. A separate pantry, with cubbies that climbed to the ceiling, made the space ideal for playing hide-and-seek. And for burying treasures. In one of those crannies lay a Harlem Renaissance painting that wouldn't emerge for another thirty years.

The children's rooms were taken over by my older brothers in the late 1950s, when the third-floor tenants moved out. Still, they were only to be used as playrooms and, later, studies. We all continued to sleep on the second floor, which remained sealed off from the rest of the house at night. I loved the musty smell of the third floor, its skylights and bright sunbeams, and the big-boy toys of my brother Alan: a seven-foot-long foldable pool table, a locomotive set with steel tracks, and an enormous red fire truck with working ladder and steering wheel. My favorite toy was a tin tractor-trailer truck just big enough for me to sit on, whose cab unhitched like the big rigs'. The back had little latch doors that swung open to load smaller cars and trucks. I used to line up these small vehicles and practice backing the trailer between them; with its cab moving in the opposite direction, the task presented quite the challenge.

Although both of our parents wanted us to have the best of everything, Mom was far more willing to pay the price. From FAO Schwarz she bought Corgi diecast collectible cars and handmade marionettes, including a replica of the one that Paul Winchell used on the *Winchell-Mahoney Time* television show. She took us to Polk's Model Craft Hobbies on Fifth Avenue, the only store in New York City with its own slot car racetrack. Each floor at Polk's was devoted to a different obsession: toy soldiers on the first; helicopter, airplane, and ship model kits, along with a complete outer-space collection, on the second; gas-powered and electric cars and trains on the fourth. Alan's Revell slot car sets and Lionel trains came from Polk's. It was also the place to buy all the parts to build custom-made vehicles. I was still too young to build my own slot cars but, on special occasions, Alan allowed me to be his helper. I felt very important being his set of tiny hands, holding a tin wire steady as he soldered it in place. Sometimes my hands would tremble for fear that I'd slip and be cast from his room.

George's room, by contrast, was a place for serious business. He was the smart son, or as Alan and I quipped, "Honorable Number One Son," mimicking the faux-Chinese accent of Detective Charlie Chan. He had completed two years of the gifted children's program at the John Peter Tetard School (Junior High School 143) in the Bronx and was now attending the prestigious private academy, the Horace Mann School, in Riverdale, New York. School had always come easily to George, but the rigor and competitiveness at Horace Mann exceeded anything he had known before. As one of a handful of blacks there, he felt even more pressure to perform. Although his years at Mann overlapped with those of the now scandalized pedophiles who taught there, George would be haunted only by the racial taunts of his classmates and football teammates—and by the occasional remark of a teacher. But, years later, when stories of sex abuse broke, he was not surprised. Teachers, headmasters, and choirmasters routinely invited select students to their homes, a practice that never raised so much as an eyebrow. One teacher took five or six kids at a time for two-week summer field trips to his lakefront property in Vermont. George had attended at least twice. For a Negro student, such an invitation signified a level of social acceptance.

George recalled Tek Young Lin, the much-loved teacher who later admitted to having sexual contact with at least three students. Lin was always trying to beautify the grounds, "but also seemed a little too interested in the boys." George had vivid memories of his English teacher Robert Berman, who enthralled his sophomore class with *Moby-Dick* and *Paradise Lost* and who would later join the list of sex predators at the school. George could still visualize this commanding yet slightly built man with the dark sunglasses and the delicate hands, which he rested on the ornate wooden arms of his high chair, positioned dead center in the classroom, as he lectured off the top of his head, never referring to notes. He called his adolescent students "his children" and warned them that they'd never understand anything without him because they lacked the intelligence and education.

"He spoke enough Latin and Italian to convince a novice he knew much more," George recalled. "Maybe he did. All the kids believed it, either way. They also believed he had a fiancée who had died mysteriously some years back, which accounted for his quirky behavior."

As much as George disliked Berman, he would always remember the one bit of advice he wished he'd taken. During George's senior year, Berman pulled him aside one day after class and told him he should get out of New York, away from the racial tensions, the civil rights strife, and the antiwar protests, and go to a small Midwestern college with a large endowment, where he could retreat and become a scholar. New York was imploding, he warned George, and it would suck him in and destroy him. It did.

In *Black Manhattan* (1930), James Weldon Johnson wrote that Harlem had all the elements of a "cosmopolitan center." Some thirty-five years later, this was still true. Most folks on our block had stable incomes, bourgeois aspirations, advanced degrees, and professional occupations. Doctors and lawyers, many from the Caribbean, lived down the street and were a part of our lives. Dr. Dobson—my baby doctor—lived two doors down. When I was six, he employed me to empty the half dozen ashtrays that dotted his small office. Dobson was an icon on the block and a noted Harlem bachelor in the society pages of *Jet* magazine (although it was rumored that the doctor kept regular company with Miss Virgie Lumpkin, the attractive nursery school director). The Rawlings lived in the corner house. They were a family of lawyers who had handled our family business for decades. Dr. Morgan and his family lived around the corner, on 145th Street toward Saint Nicholas Avenue; other doctors had home offices up on 148th toward Amsterdam Avenue. In fact, growing up, I was surrounded by doctors and lawyers.

Our housekeeper, Mrs. Grandberry, doubled as my nanny until I was eight. Every morning we worked out with Jack LaLanne, doing jumping jacks and knee lifts and stretching with our giant rubber bands while he chided us for letting our bustlines go. Saturday mornings meant *Winky Dink and You*, hosted by Jack Barry. *Winky Dink* required a special kit—a clear plastic overlap (called a "magic TV window") that fit over the television, along with erasable crayons to draw in a rope or ladder or bridge to rescue Winky from the next jam. It was the world's first touchscreen video.

Television had yet to outgrow its demeaning stereotypes of black people. Jack Benny's butler, Rochester, was still shuffling, and Buckwheat was TV's favorite pickaninny. Bill Cosby, who had been regularly appearing in *I Spy* since 1960, was the one authentic black person that white people regularly allowed into their living rooms. Others, like Louis, Ella, or the Duke, were honored guests on *The Ed Sullivan Show*, and we were all rallied to the set whenever they appeared. This was a period when black identity was in flux. Older folk, like my parents, still referred to themselves as Negroes, while my brothers were black, proud, and beautiful. By the time King was shot, everyone in Harlem was black.

My parents entertained regularly in the early days. Smoke-filled evenings were tinted with gin and scotch poured into hand-painted, gold-rimmed Italian tumblers with matching stirrers, fruit cocktails topped with maraschino cherries served in Waterford glass bowls, and festive finger sandwiches made with red- and green-dyed bread.

Dolly and her elderly gentleman friend Dr. Edgehill were frequent guests, as was my mother's friend Lillian Benton—a fellow social worker and Alpha Kappa Alpha sister—and the Johnsons, who lived downtown in a white neighborhood. Clarence Johnson was light-skinned like my father, but his wife, Ethel, confused me. She seemed white. Visible in the backs of her hands were blue veins, which only white people seemed to have. Still, she was far too comfortable with black folk not to be black. For years I remained in doubt about Ethel's race. No one in the family ever talked about it or seemed to care.

By 1958, nearly a third of all adults in the country played bridge, and millions belonged to regular card clubs. Bridge signified status, that one had time for leisure. Indeed, the very act of entertaining—bringing out the English bone china, the crystal stemware, and the sterling silver—allowed the middle class to demonstrate that it was middle class. In 1955, when E. Franklin Frazier— the first black president of the American Sociological Association and one of the leading scholars on American race relations—indicted the black bourgeoisie for reproducing the conventions of white society, he underestimated the long-term effect that group activities such as bridge and bowling would have on building community and reinforcing social ties.

Bridge soirees were a familiar scene in our home, until entertaining there was no longer an option. The end began when I was six and my mother discovered that Pop had previously been married. (I later learned that he'd actually been married twice before, although I don't believe my mother ever got wind of the second marriage.)

Pop clearly never had any intention of telling her, but he must have considered the likelihood that she'd uncover it on her own. He kept the divorce papers stashed away in a wooden cigar box in the bottom drawer of his file cabinet, along with the bankbooks, financial statements, and other personal documents he meant to keep away from her. And though he always locked the cabinet, we all knew where he hid the key—on a nail just inside the closet door. Perhaps he assumed she abided by the same code that he did and would never pry into his private affairs.

For Mom, perhaps the key alone signified that Pop had something to hide. Or perhaps she was simply curious about how much money they had accumulated. In keeping with the conventions of the 1950s and 1960s, Daisy always handed over her weekly paycheck to her husband, who then doled out a carefully budgeted household allowance. How much had they saved by now? Was money really as tight as he claimed? And what was this yellow envelope buried under the passbooks?

Daisy let the tension build slowly. Over the coming weeks, she made vague insinuations, cryptic little digs about the sanctity of their marriage. George, sixteen now, finally asked what was going on. It took that little puff to blow the house down. George could still recite the exchange forty years later.

"Ed Haynes! You've been hiding something from me!"

"I don't know what you're talking about," he protested.

"Yeah, you do. You were married before, weren't you?"

He'd had twenty years to prepare his response, but when the moment came, he faltered like a schoolboy.

"Daisy . . . uh . . . I had a few too many one night and got conned into it."

She scoffed at his feeble excuses and cowardice. Here he stood now, this man who had held himself above reproach, who had chastised her for bringing home a stapler from work—"State property," he declared—while withholding the most fundamental of truths for almost twenty years.

Although I later came to question how a youthful transgression could unravel a happy marriage, the simple right and wrong of it made sense to a boy of six. It also meant, as my nanny assured me, that it had nothing to do with me. Now I question that, too. Born seven years after Alan and ten years after George, I came as more than a surprise to my mother. I came as an effrontery. When she learned she was pregnant, she confided to George, not quite ten, that she didn't know how she had "ever let that happen" and that she was furious with Pop for "shackling her down with another baby." (To her credit, she never made me feel unwanted.) So maybe the discovery of Pop's marriage was just kindling for a smoldering fire. Or maybe it represented a breach of propriety, which mattered a great deal to my parents' generation. Whatever the reason, they never examined it together.

Although they returned to the semblance of normalcy over the next few weeks, Daisy's wounds festered. She became unrelenting, excoriating Pop for his duplicity, goading him on as he fended her off. She meant to badger him into abandoning that self-restraint she had once so admired. One morning, she finally penetrated his armor. He picked up a bottle of Zestabs chewable vitamins from the breakfast table and hurled it through the double-pane window.

The window was never repaired, nor was anything else that broke or shattered or collapsed thereafter. Looking back, I realize that this was the moment that our house began its decline, the crash of the glass a knell for what was yet to come.

♥

The decline would be gradual. For the first few years, we still had Mrs. Grandberry, who cleaned and dusted, vacuumed and polished, and shielded me from the chaos erupting all around us. I often went home with her on weekends, perhaps at my parents' urging, or at least to their relief. She lived in Harlem's valley, in a dreary cold-water flat that she heated by turning on the oven and boiling pots of water. Mrs. Grandberry was a devout Seventh-day Adventist and the first to expose me to religion. She taught me to say grace and to recite the Lord's Prayer—at noontime and bedtime. She gave me my first Bible and taught me to take nothing for granted. Whenever her family parted ways, they'd pray, "May the Lord watch between me and thee while we're absent one from another." I often attended church with her on the Sabbath, at the Ephesus Seventh-day Adventist Church on West 123rd Street, just around the corner from her house.

When Mrs. Grandberry retired, in 1968, the shine and luster of our home departed with her. My mother refused to do housework and my father retaliated by becoming more miserly, refusing to spend money on repairs and applying his own rudimentary skills to any crisis, big or small. Leaks in the roof were repaired in patchwork. Paint and plaster peeled, pipes corroded. Things that broke were simply saved for repair—at some distant day in the future. When the television console broke down, it became a stand for the new portable transistor television from Sony that had taken the market by storm. Eventually the kitchen plumbing on the second floor was repaired, but the walls were never replastered, leaving exposed the wire mesh and water pipes behind the sink. A gaping hole festered for the next thirty years. The hole slowly blended in with the rest of the tiny kitchen, whose construction had been ill planned when the house was converted to three family units, back in the 1950s. No ventilation hood had been built over the stove, and the once yellow walls and cabinets were darkened with coats of dust and grease.

Meanwhile, Daisy went shopping, running up my father's charge cards to even the score. She had always been extravagant—I had a cashmere suit when I was four—but now she shopped with a vengeance. Every Saturday morning, Daisy would make the hajj to midtown Manhattan, prostrating herself before the newest collections of women's high-end apparel. During the fifties and early sixties, she had frequented B. Altman, the first major department store on Fifth Avenue, along with Stern's department store on 42nd Street and E. J. Korvette, a discount store with middle-class appeal at Herald Square. Occasionally she dropped by Saks Fifth Avenue, whose hallowed entryway transported her to paradise itself. But as Daisy's marriage soured, her tastes became pricier and she began shopping almost exclusively along Fifth Avenue. Though Bergdorf Goodman was where she bought her clothes for work (for stodgy women's clothing with an "old money" feeling, Bergdorf was the place), Saks had the style and the social scene—the beauty parlor and nail salon where Jewish women met and talked about their children. Daisy could *kvell* with the best of them, and for years she kept a standing Saturday appointment with her manicurist, Tina, at the Saks salon.

She made quite the statement, strolling down Fifth Avenue with her black, custom-designed mink coat and dazzling rings. This short, stout woman —all but five foot one and a healthy one hundred fifty pounds—always appeared in full makeup, with long, deep red nails, whose many coats of paint sparkled like a Corvette straight off the assembly line.

On these beautiful soft hands that belied her age sat a fat gold bauble with tiny stone insets that took up most of her middle knuckle. Next to the bauble lay a simple, tasteful gold ring. Her wedding band and engagement ring—a big rock—occupied her index finger. She defied the odds for years, riding the subways and walking through Harlem, gold baubles and all, and was never mugged. Her mink coat, which set Pop back a cool $5,000—a fortune in those days—was bought from Mr. Ritter's shop, the fancy furrier downtown. She broke it out on Saturdays and for special occasions. (Once, my mother's mink saved her from breaking her neck. She was walking down the subway stairs when she slipped and started tumbling. Ensconced in thick fur, she literally bounced down the stairs to safety!) She wore her fancy gold pins and a men's gold pocket watch around her neck until her dying day.

It wasn't just that Daisy wanted to look good. Dressing up was a prerequisite in a city where, barely a decade earlier, middle-class black folk couldn't even try on clothing in certain stores. Black salesclerks were still a rarity in midtown department stores, and black shoppers were even fewer.

Daisy represented a new breed of black middle-class women who came of age just after the war. These aspiring cosmopolitans broke with the stifling conventions of church and temperance of their mothers' generation. They grew up on the glamour of Hollywood movies, wore makeup and high heels, and openly smoked cigarettes in public (though never in front of their mothers). They were educated and sophisticated. They shopped downtown by day and danced at the Savoy with their husbands by night. They spoke Standard English while they listened to Ray Charles and Solomon Burke, Oscar Peterson and Bobby Short, Ella Fitzgerald and Billie Holiday.

Unlike their postwar white counterparts, black middle-class women tended to work. Many worked out of financial necessity, because their husbands' jobs—as porters or clerks (good jobs for a black man), or as professionals in segregated settings—earned little. Others worked because their identities as black women depended on it. Like the generation of educated black women before them, they often viewed their work as a vehicle for advancing the race. For them, race responsibility and equal rights were entwined—equal rights in terms of race, that is, not gender. They didn't identify with the grievances of well-to-do white women whose husbands wouldn't allow them to work. Nor did they regard work as a means to attain gender equality, although in the long run it did deliver a degree of economic independence. Black middle-class women would come to embody the first "super-moms" that America produced. Not only did they cook and raise their children, just as their mothers had done before them, but also this generation of women would be the first to have professional careers in traditional middle-class occupations. They'd be the first to work in truly integrated settings and to demand respect from their white peers as well as their partners. In the late 1960s, when the City of New York created the Department of Health and Mental Hygiene, Daisy became one of the principal evaluators of mental health programs and children's services at the city's major hospitals. By the seventies, she was a program analyst in her office on the eightieth floor of the World Trade Center—Tower 2 (where she and I watched the tall ships parading through New York Harbor during America's bicentennial). She was proud and commanded respect wherever she went.

Her makeup, hair, nails, shoes, handbags, jewelry and, above all, her attitude said that she was somebody, and whites responded accordingly. She could disarm the most hardened of racists with her southern graces, but she was nobody's "handkerchief head"— a southernism she was fond of—and wouldn't hesitate to put a white man in his place with a few choice words.

The saleswomen downtown adored her. They held her packages behind the counter while she shopped. They called her at home if an unadvertised sale was being planned. They even let her use their special employee discounts, purchasing the items themselves and holding them until she returned later in the week to retrieve them—always bringing a little box of assorted *rugelach* from Zabar's to show her appreciation.

Her children became part of her entourage. Back in the 1950s, George and Alan used to accompany Daisy on her shopping ventures, once they were old enough to carry packages. She insisted that they dress in a suit and tie for these trips, even in the dead of summer. They sported argyle socks, bow ties, and little dark blue blazers as they trudged behind her dutifully through the department stores, standing straight and alert as she stopped to test a new perfume or try on a smart French scarf. They didn't

mind these trips when they were young; this was Daisy's world
and it was magical. I came along just in time to take their place,
when their interests shifted to sports, girls, and music. Every
Saturday morning, my mother would dress me up in khakis and
a polo shirt like a proper little man of leisure.

Trips downtown with Daisy meant presents for us—a radio, a
chess set, walkie-talkies, clothes. And we'd almost always stop
along the way for a special treat, like a hot dog and Coke at
Nedick's or an ice cream soda at Schrafft's. Sometimes we'd trek
all the way to Third Avenue and 42nd Street to what became the
last Horn & Hardart Automat in New York City. Despite its
high-tech name, the Automat was strangely mechanical and
archaic. In fact, nothing was really automated at all. It operated
on the same principle as a gumball machine. You dropped your
nickels and dimes in the slot and turned the knob that released a
latch. And just as you lifted the little glass door to remove your
package, a little hand emerged from the back to replenish the
shelf. It was all a little cheesy. Most people preferred to maintain
the illusion that they were engaged in some cutting-edge exchange. Yet there was something nostalgic and comforting about
the Automat. Here you could enjoy a slice of apple pie on a nice
china plate for a few cents, or a hot cup of coffee in a real cup—
fast food with a dash of Old World charm. Retired veterans
from the Great War whiled away their final days in the booths
with their coffees and newspapers.

The place I loved best was Chock full o'Nuts. The whiff of
warm frankfurters bolstered your soul on a cold winter day. So
did the ladies behind the counter—middle-aged black women in
hairnets and white rubber-soled orthopedic shoes, addressing
you as "Honey" or "Sweetie." Daisy always ordered a coffee and
the Chock Classic—a date-nut bread and cream cheese sandwich—for herself, and a frank with mustard, a Coke, and a sugar

doughnut—the powdery kind that crumbled onto the counter and all of my clothes—for me.

Another favorite spot was Patricia Murphy's, right across from Saks, on 49th Street, where fat popovers bulged and burst with intoxicating puffs of steam. Service came with linen napkins and fancy silverware. Crème de menthe was served over crushed ice for dessert. It was a place where cups had saucers and smartly dressed boys were addressed by waitresses as "young men." I was the perfect escort for the dazzling lady who sat across from me.

Being with my mother was like being at the center of the universe. Everyone knew and loved Miss Daisy, as they called her, and treated her like a queen. She had the airs and manners of a grand lady, a Southern belle, and she carried herself like royalty. But, at the end of the day, shopping was no salve for the soured marriage she returned to.

Pop displeased her so. The reserve and propriety that once attested his pedigree now signaled a lack of gumption. She saw herself as a mover and shaker, pushing free into the wide universe of New York's black elite. When she wasn't shopping downtown, she was carving out her social network uptown, hobnobbing with jazz musicians and immersing herself in Harlem's burgeoning artistic movement. Unlike my father, who eschewed the trappings of the black bourgeoisie, Daisy cultivated the social ties that came with it, and she served on the boards of several Harlem-based cultural institutions that were founded during this period, such as the Dance Theatre of Harlem and the AMAS Repertory Theatre—the multiracial company founded in 1968 by actress-producer Rosetta LeNoire.

Rosetta was one of the few people Daisy really looked up to. Familiar to most post–baby boomers as Nell Carter's mother in the 1980s NBC sitcom *Gimme a Break!* and, later, as Mother

Winslow in *Family Matters*, Rosetta had once been an acclaimed stage actress. As a young girl, she had studied piano with the jazz great Eubie Blake and tap-danced with Bill "Bojangles" Robinson. Born Rosetta Burton, she later reinvented herself with a Frenchified stage name, becoming Rosetta LeNoire—"Rosetta the Black." Her debut came in 1935, when Orson Welles pulled her out of a Lower East Side company to place her in a Harlem production of *Macbeth*—set in Haiti—and cast her as the First Witch. In 1939, she made her Broadway debut in the all-black operetta *Hot Mikado*, playing alongside her godfather, Bojangles. By the 1970s, she resurrected Eubie Blake in the AMAS production *Reminiscing with Sissle and Blake* and, later, in the Broadway hit *Bubbling Brown Sugar*.

Rosetta's efforts resuscitated the arts of the Jazz Age, making it possible for a new generation of tap dancers, such as Ben Vereen and Savion Glover, to perform for a thriving audience. She single-handedly revived an entire generation of black theater that had too often been regarded as shucking and jiving and thus had been reviled by many in the new black cultural arts movement. Through AMAS, Rosetta provided neighborhood kids in all shades of brown with opportunities to study music and the arts. I studied guitar there briefly, in 1968, when the center was still at its original location—a large room inside an old church on East 101st Street, in Spanish Harlem. The room was cordoned off with fake walls to make an office, where Daisy and Rosetta would talk while I took my lessons just outside. The tiny quarters of AMAS rang with blues, jazz, gospel, and ragtime. I met patrons of the arts, performers from the vaudeville era, tap dancers from the twenties and, once, Mr. Eubic Blake himself. (Some thirty years later, when I was clearing out the house, I found tomes of AMAS literature, instruments, and furniture, and even a portable electric generator that had been placed in our safekeeping while the theater was transitioning from its cramped quarters in Spanish Harlem to its new location in Greenwich Village.)

With my mother out socializing much of the time, I became a faithful companion to my father, tagging along with him on his household chores. In our home's division of labor, laundry was Pop's territory. He would grab his old folding shopping cart, the rectangular, two-wheeled kind commonly used by the poor and aged for carting goods around the city, and together we'd carry the clothes a block and a half up the hill to Amsterdam Avenue, where Mr. Hatcher's Laundromat stood. We actually still had two washing machines in the house, but neither worked. Rather than buy a new machine, which my parents could well have afforded, Pop opted to "save money" by sinking untold numbers of quarters into Mr. Hatcher's machines, every week for the rest of his life.

Commerce in the Heights was concentrated between 140th and 147th Streets, along Broadway, Saint Nicholas, and Amsterdam Avenues. There, one could be in any small town in America, with its mom-and-pop groceries, stationery stores, shoe repair shops, and dry cleaners. Small clothing and hardware stores bore the names of their Italian and Jewish owners—some warm and avuncular, others who treated you like a criminal. Pop's barber, Renée, was on Broadway, at West 145th Street, across the street from Copeland's, the upscale soul food establishment where Stevie Wonder, Harry Belafonte, and Sammy Davis Jr. had once been regulars and where my mom sometimes treated us to a slice of sweet potato pie. Pop's idea of a treat was the fifteen-cent popcorn at the Woolworths next door.

Pop was my best pal for years. I couldn't go out to play, because the streets were becoming unsafe, but he showed me the world. He took me to the American Museum of Natural History, where, in 1969, we saw the new installation of the blue whale. He took me to Jones Beach and Shea Stadium in Queens (although we lived within walking distance of Yankee Stadium, Pop would never forgive the New York Yankees for being slow to recruit black ballplayers), to the Bronx Zoo and the New York Botanical Garden, to Saturday matinees at Radio City Music Hall, and to Ringling Bros. and Barnum & Bailey Circus at Madison Square Garden. Of course, there would never be popcorn or candy or soda, unless we were lucky enough to pass a five-and-dime store along the way.

We were all shocked when he came home one day with a brand-new 1966 Chrysler Newport four-door hardtop. The Newport was Chrysler's lowest-priced model, but still! Chrysler signified class, as its ads informed us: "Move up to Chrysler." "You're probably in the Chrysler class right now—and don't even know it." He even rented a space at the garage down the street, a former stable with two white horse heads in relief above the entry way.

Pop was the driver other drivers never wanted to be stuck behind. He'd coast the last couple of hundred yards to the stop sign, manually downshifting the automatic transmission from drive to second gear. "Saving my breaks," he'd boast with a big smile. Whatever Pop was doing, he was saving, even when he was spending. But, for all his thriftiness, he never questioned spending money on our education and, later, on private psychiatric care for George. He reminded us constantly of the importance of education and hard work, even before I started school. Hard work had a different meaning for black folk. "You need to earn an A if you expect to get a B," he would tell us. We always knew what we were up against.

♥

My parents never spoke about divorce but resigned themselves to a lifetime of tiny assaults and retreats. Lulls were charged with icy silence and punctuated with bitter rebukes, usually hers. "Oh,

Ed, no one's asking what you think!" He grew quiet but patiently waited for her to muddle an idiom—a frequent occurrence—or to slip up on a point of grammar. "You don't express yourself well, Daisy Mae," he'd coolly observe. He had attended the best schools, come from the world she aspired to, and was well aware that this remark would knock her down a peg or two.

Still, Pop rejected much of the bourgeois society she had married into, and he couldn't care less about how he looked. To my mother's horror, he took to wearing his moth-eaten World War II jacket when lounging about the house or sitting on the front stoop. His favorite pants had a busted zipper and were held together with a safety pin. He looked like he could have been a homeless person. Yet his diction and phrasing were strictly upper crust.

My mother picked at him constantly. "Straighten your tie, Ed." "Take off that shirt, Ed Haynes. Can't you see it's got a stain on it?" "Oh, no! You're not thinking about wearing *that*, are you?" I cringed when she berated him in public. "Lord have mercy, Ed! Push that plate up on the table before your food ends up in your lap!" Pop feigned the browbeaten husband while steadily nudging his plate to the edge. Sometimes he'd pipe up and show a little spunk. "You're running at the mouth, Daisy," was one of his better rejoinders.

The subject of money was a predictable trigger. Pop's penny pinching—he'd travel miles out of his way to avoid a toll and was a conservationist way before it was fashionable, grilling us whenever we left a light on ("Do you think we own Con Edison?")—belied his privileged beginnings. Daisy, with her humble Carolina roots, burned the candle at both ends. To her, life was meant to be lived. "I never saw a Brinks trunk following a hearse," she'd declare triumphantly. Any pacts they had made at the start of their marriage were null and void, as far as she was concerned. The rift between what he felt they could afford and what she felt entitled to spend was played out every Saturday, when she returned from a day of downtown shopping. Each exchange seemed to begin and end in the same way. Only the token gift for my father varied from one week to the next.

"Daisy, I hope you didn't put all this on the charge card."

"Well, I don't know how else you thought I was going to pay for it!"

"I told you we can't be running up the bills. We're trying to save a little bit so we can have a little bit."

"Well, the holidays are coming and Alan and Brucie need shoes and you needed batteries for your flashlight. I stopped by Duane Reade. See? And then they had this sale, so I just picked up a couple of things."

"A couple of things? You've got five bags here!"

"Don't worry about it. I'll pay you back!"

"What do you mean, pay me back? You've put it on a charge card, and you're still paying me back from the last time."

"But look at the shirt I bought you."

This was her ace in the hole. He looked it over and had to admit it was pretty nice.

"I can take it back if you like. Give it to me. I'll take it back!" She knew she had him now. "I can take it right back downtown. I'm sure they'll be plenty glad to take it back."

"Well, alright, Daisy Mae, just this one time."

George, who once believed Pop was invincible, who marveled at his large strong hands and his Smith & Wesson .38 Special, was furious to see him succumb so easily to our mother. He was often sullen and aloof, which our parents dismissed as normal teenage behavior. But he was also finding it difficult to focus. He began struggling in classes he'd once sailed through, and his grades at Horace Mann slipped. Our parents only magnified his sense of failure, vying for his sympathies, turning to him to mediate their arguments.

Eventually, he pushed for the three of them to begin family therapy. They responded by sending him, alone, to a bearded psychiatrist on East 68th Street, who was long on the psychobabble but came up short on a diagnosis.

Daisy's therapy was retail. She began spending even more time away from home and more money on herself. Whatever cash and plastic she couldn't get Pop to part with, she made up for with her *sou-sou* account. An obscure savings system said to have originated in Africa, *sou-sou* was handed down from generation to generation and was still popular among women of my mother's generation. The rules are simple: each member contributes a set amount for a set period of time. At the end of the period, one person collects all the money. The cycle continues until everyone gets a "hand." The system was commonly practiced among poor blacks and Caribbean immigrants—who were often charged higher interest rates to borrow money—in order to make a down payment on a house, launch a business, or finance other sizeable investments. Now it became another source of Daisy's mad money.

2

NOT ALMS BUT OPPORTUNITY

NLIKE my mother, who aspired to be a respected member of the black bourgeoisie, my father was born into it. Yet he had been a lonely boy, the son of two accomplished and driven careerists. His mother, Elizabeth Ross Haynes ("Rossi," as the family called her), worked right through his childhood. And although she was a distinguished children's author of the Harlem Renaissance, a respected scholar on female domestic labor, a researcher for the federal government, and a fervent social activist and politician, she always lived in the shadow of her more illustrious husband. Rarely paid for her work, she worked tirelessly nonetheless and spent little time at home. Meanwhile, his father, George Edmund Haynes (or "Pop Haynes," as the family called him), was a leading scholar of the Great Migration and the founder of the National Urban League—a critical anchor for the millions of rural southern Negroes migrating to the urban industrial North. George and Rossi's social circle included such Harlem Renaissance luminaries as Alain Locke (the philosopher and writer), Langston Hughes, Countee Cullen, and the preeminent scholar and civil rights activist of the early twentieth century, W. E. B. Du Bois.

Du Bois was the leading black intellectual of his day. In 1899, he wrote the first empirical study of an American city—*The Philadelphia Negro*. Four years later, he published his seminal treatise on race, *The Souls of Black Folk*, which took on Booker T. Washington's accommodationist stance on segregation and offered a vision of an American society unencumbered by race. Du Bois was also a cofounder of the National Association for the Advancement of Colored People (NAACP) and a political strategist of the Harlem Renaissance. Today he is recognized as one of the founding fathers of American sociology and the first to establish it as a scientific discipline. He produced the first generation of black social scientists, including Richard R. Wright, Monroe Work, and George E. Haynes.

Du Bois was the single greatest influence on my grandfather's life. From Haynes's early days in high school, Du Bois shaped his scholarship and career choices. He brought Haynes into his intellectual network, counseled him at pivotal junctures in his career, and continually advocated for his professional advancement. The two men would remain close friends and confidants throughout their lives, even as Du Bois lost hope in the vision they had once shared.

When I was growing up, my father rarely spoke about the family patriarch. He referred to Pop Haynes as merely an "educator" and mentioned only in passing that W. E. B. Du Bois used to visit the house. Although Pop was proud of his father's accomplishments, he always had a nagging sense that he had been a disappointment to his father, that he could have been more. Even with his father's portrait buried safely in the attic, the towering figure loomed large above him all his life, reminding him of his own smallness.

As a result of my father's silence on the subject, most of what I came to know about my grandfather was through books. The record shows that George Edmund Haynes was a light-skinned

Negro who stood barely five foot eight in his stocking feet and weighed in at one hundred fifty pounds. He might have passed for a Cuban, with his olive skin, finely chiseled features, and dark curly locks. Despite his parents' humble background—his mother, Mattie Sloan Haynes, was a domestic worker, and his father, Louis Haynes, was an unskilled seasonal laborer—the family owned property in Pine Bluff, Arkansas, at least as early as 1880, when George Haynes was born. I never learned how this Negro family came to own property in the segregated Southwest just fifteen years after slavery, but the seed of our family's success was planted on that land.

George was first educated in Pine Bluff's local, segregated school system where, in accordance with an 1867 state law, a free public school education was available only to whites. Louis and Mattie scraped by on their meager wages to pay the special tax to send George and his younger sister, Birdye, to a one-room schoolhouse for Negro boys and girls. After Louis died, Mattie sold the property and moved the family to Hot Springs, Arkansas, which offered better schools and job opportunities. By fifteen, George was enrolled in the college preparatory program of the State Agricultural and Mechanical College for Negroes, in Normal, Alabama. A year later, he transferred to the more elite preparatory program at Fisk University, in Nashville, Tennessee. There he met the renowned Negro scholar and orator W. E. B. Du Bois, who had also attended Fisk and was now returning to give the commencement address to the 1898 graduating class. Du Bois would soon become George's mentor and make key connections for him, eventually advocating for his leadership in the highest of offices.

The atmosphere at historically black colleges was steeped in their Christian roots. A Bible was required in every room, and a litany of activities was forbidden: drinking alcohol, smoking tobacco, using profanity, playing cards, betting, gambling, and even dancing. Yet Fisk also instilled race consciousness in its students and encouraged them to link their individual achievements to the advancement of all Negroes. In his valedictory address, George asserted that "every race or nation that has gained a place of high virtue and power has done so through the sacrifice of its best and brightest men and women," and that "this class of the race must sacrifice itself to uplift the rest of the race." The idea was gaining momentum in Du Bois's call for a "Talented Tenth."

That next fall, George began graduate studies at Yale University, studying with William G. Sumner, a laissez-faire economist and one of the most influential figures in early American sociology. Sumner was a staunch advocate of individual liberty and an opponent of most social reforms—he even opposed giving Negroes the right to vote. Drawing on Darwin's theories of evolution, he argued,

> The sociologist is often asked if he wants to kill off certain classes of troublesome and bewildered persons. No such interference follows from any sound sociological doctrine, but it is allowed to infer, as to a great many persons and classes, that it would have been better for society and would have involved no pain to them, if they had never been born.

It must have seemed like an impossible challenge for my grandfather to demonstrate his worth to Sumner. He would have had to demonstrate that he was smarter than any of his white peers while being careful not to appear too smart or too big for his britches.

Sumner's attitude was typical of the times. In these early days at Yale, Negro students were questioned on their qualifications, and most were required to complete a second bachelor's degree before entering graduate school. According to an unpublished memoir, when George tried to register for a course in experimental psychology, the professor told him, "You graduates from these southern Negro colleges have not had adequate training to meet the strenuous requirements of graduate courses at Yale." George proved him wrong, completing his master's degree in one year, after which the dean informed him that he'd overcome his "handicap." I imagine that George would be tickled to learn that his lifework would one day be housed in some of the top university libraries in the country, including Yale's own Beinecke Rare Book & Manuscript Library.

That next year, George enrolled in Yale Divinity School, but after conferring with Du Bois, he left the program and accepted a position with the YMCA. Du Bois was skeptical of white church leaders and believed that the race problem existed as much within the church as outside it. Although the YMCA maintained segregated practices, its sheer size and reach led Du Bois to conclude, in a letter to my grandfather, that the position offered "greater possibilities than that open to a Congregational minister. The development of sufficient moral forces outside the churches to compel the churches to change face is the problem before us." George took the job with the YMCA, working first in the Colored Men's Department of the Atlanta office, and later as a traveling student secretary.

Long before the YMCA became associated with cheap rooms and cheap sex, it provided a Christian-influenced environment for single men: Bible study, physical fitness, and a safe place to rest your head. It was the male counterpart of the women's settlement house movement, a place of temperance and Christian values, a refuge for decent, hardworking men of the nineteenth-century metropolis. At the outbreak of the Civil War, the New York YMCA added job placement to its list of services, providing employers with a morally wholesome and trustworthy workforce.

During the summers, George took courses at the University of Chicago, which was one of the more welcoming schools for Negro students. Unlike many institutions of the period, it did not require prospective graduate students to submit certificates from accredited colleges—a practice that disproportionately affected black students, because few Negro colleges were accredited at the time. Most important, the University of Chicago was already becoming known as the place where promising Negro scholars could study with the top social scientists of the day, such as Albion Small, who headed the first department of sociology at the school.

After three years with the YMCA, George returned to his studies, enrolling in the New York School of Philanthropy. He was interested in exploring the economic conditions of blacks in New York City, and Du Bois arranged an introduction with Mary White Ovington—the wealthy white suffragette (and eventual cofounder of the NAACP) who was studying the lives of Negroes in the North. George gained the attention of Edward T. Devine, the head of the Bureau of Applied Social Research and director of the social research department at Columbia University, who helped him gain admission to Columbia's doctoral program in social economics. Over the next two years, George studied under some of the most preeminent social scientists of the day, including the American economist Edwin R. A. Seligman, and applied economics and sociology to understanding the migration patterns of southern blacks.

Most social scientists saw the growing numbers of southern Negro migrants as a temporary phenomenon and focused on rural solutions like agricultural training to curb their flow. But George's research showed that the movement from the rural South to the urban North was part of a broader shift, among both whites and blacks, from agriculture toward the new industrial economies—"pull factors." Yet he also identified "push factors" that applied to blacks only: discrimination, segregation, the inequities of sharecropping, and the persistent threat of mob violence (which George termed "anti-Negro terrorism"). His analysis of migratory patterns—using a push-pull model—was remarkably sophisticated for the period. As one scholar later put it, "More modern theories of migration exhibit remarkably little advance over Haynes' conception." One hundred years later, Isabel Wilkerson, the author of *The Warmth of Other Suns*, would call the Great Migration the biggest unreported story of the twentieth century. My grandfather not only foresaw the Great Migration that was about to unfold but also went on to create the very structures and supports that would spur the continued flow of migrants into New York, Chicago, and many other urban centers in the North and Midwest. In the end, though, he was relegated to a footnote in history, and sometimes less than that, as witnessed by Wilkerson's book.

By the time he graduated, in 1912—becoming the first person of African descent to receive a doctorate from Columbia University—George Haynes had founded the second most important civil rights institution in the nation's history. The first, of course, was the NAACP, founded in 1910 by W. E. B. Du Bois and Mary White Ovington, which used the twin strategies of political agitation and legal action to fight Jim Crow segregation and violence against Negroes. What was needed now, as George saw it, was a comprehensive program to provide education, training, and jobs for the growing number of Negro migrants in New York and other northern cities.

He conferred with Du Bois, along with his old professors and the sociologist Frances Kellor, but received the greatest support from the philanthropist and social reformer Ruth Standish Baldwin, who was deeply committed to the rights and welfare of Negro migrants. Together, they founded the National League on Urban Conditions Among Negroes, in 1911 (renamed the

National Urban League in 1919). Baldwin—along with John D. Rockefeller Jr., Alfred T. White, and Julius Rosenwald, the president of Sears, Roebuck and Company—provided the financial ties. George brought the vision: economic empowerment as a vehicle for social change.

Before the days of the Works Progress Administration— the signature New Deal program under President Franklin D. Roosevelt—a man without a job was on his own, and children and widows were no better off. Negroes were accustomed to making do; there was no government dole yet, and what little social support existed was largely barred to Negroes. Cities were becoming inundated with the homeless, spawning the mission and settlement house movements and the development of poor farms and poorhouses—publicly run residences where the destitute, homeless, and disabled were housed. The league's manifesto— "Not alms but opportunity"—captured the spirit of the day.

My grandfather and Du Bois met early on to strategize ways to coordinate and distinguish the missions of their respective organizations: the NAACP would use open confrontation, the league, persuasion. The softer tactics of the league—through vocational guidance, policy advocacy, negotiations with industry leaders, and research to refute the prevailing social Darwinist views on the Negro—were a key advantage for the NAACP. Mary White Ovington later described this arrangement:

> Most fortunately, about six months after we began, the Urban League was formed. George Haynes, sociologist from Fisk University, came into our office one morning with plans to form a national organization in the fields of employment and of philanthropy. . . . Some of us gasped at having so large a field of "advancement" taken out of our program, but nothing could have been more fortunate. We could not have raised money for "phi-

lanthropy" as successfully as an organization with a less militant program, and securing employment is a business in itself.

The favor my grandfather curried through the league's softer, conciliatory stance, and, later, in his role as broker between Negro artists and white art patrons, would in time relegate him to the position of a middleman in history. When narratives on black institution building and the Harlem Renaissance were later told, the radical politics of the left were in fashion in academia. Du Bois would be rediscovered by a new generation of post–Civil Rights scholars and emerge as the central actor in the story. Other seminal figures, like George Haynes, would be overshadowed. Of course, Du Bois's political trajectory—as an agitator who becomes too radical for the institution he helped to found (the NAACP), joins the Communist Party, renounces his U.S. citizenship, and emigrates to Africa—made a better story, certainly more gripping than that of a man who quietly and patiently chisels away at segregation, never losing his faith or surrendering his vision.

But perhaps there was more. Although Du Bois had a bolder vision from the start, my grandfather was certainly more progressive than Booker T. Washington, whose philosophy of accommodation to segregation was embraced by southern whites. Yet Washington would go on to be remembered, even if not always kindly. Perhaps it was the middle ground Haynes occupied—neither too defiant nor compliant—that diminished his significance over time. As one historian summed him up, "Haynes was a moderate leader, more militant than Booker T. Washington but not as strident as W. E. B. Du Bois."

My grandfather certainly contemplated his posterity. Over the years, he meticulously compiled clippings of every event, big or small, at which he was honored, every speech that he gave, and every article that he published. Then again, perhaps he suspected that if he did not document his legacy, he would disappear completely. Such concerns would not be unfounded. Eugene Kinckle Jones, Haynes's successor as executive director of the National Urban League, would later write Haynes out of the organization's founding history, crediting Ruth Baldwin alone as the league's founder.

▼

Just as the league was being launched, George married Rossi. The two seemed mirrors of each other. She, too, was a migrant from the rural South—Lowndes County, Alabama. Her parents, like George's, were former slaves who had managed to acquire land in the early postwar years. Her father, Henry Ross, had run away at the outbreak of the Civil War and, like some 178,000 other Negroes, enlisted in the Union Army. By war's end, he had earned enough money to buy a small plot of land in Mount Willing, Alabama, not far from his birthplace in Letohatchee. At the dawn of freedom, few Negroes owned more than the shirt on their backs, but the wages earned by the tens of thousands who fought for the Union and their own freedom provided a foothold in the American dream, allowing some to purchase land and eventually send their children to college. After decades of toil, Rossi's parents had expanded the land into a 1,500-acre plantation.

George and Rossi had taken a common path. They had been classmates at Fisk University and graduated in the same year, 1903. They attended summer sessions at the University of Chicago, worked as student secretaries for the YMCA, and were committed to social reform and racial uplift. By all accounts, she was the intellectual equal to her husband, but while George received a scholarship to graduate school, first at Yale and later at Columbia, Rossi supported herself as a schoolteacher. Gender differences in course requirements at Fisk meant that female students would need to supplement their degrees with additional undergraduate-level courses before entering graduate school. It's not surprising, then, that many took twice as long as their male counterparts to earn advanced degrees. Two decades would pass before Rossi earned a master's degree in sociology from Columbia University. Her 1923 thesis, *Negroes in Domestic Service in the United States* (published in *The Journal of Negro History*), was the most comprehensive study of black women in America until the 1970s.

My father, George Edmund Jr. (known as Edmund), was born two years into their marriage. At the time, the family lived on West 134th Street, between Seventh and Eighth Avenues—in Harlem's valley and the very heart of the new, black Harlem. It would be another decade before middle-class blacks like my grandparents began moving into the sprawling row houses and elegantly appointed apartments up on Convent and Edgecombe Avenues, an area that came to be known as Sugar Hill, signifying the "sweet life."

Over the first six years of his life, Edmund saw very little of his father, who divided his time between the New York office of the National Urban League—serving as its first executive secretary—and Fisk University, in Nashville, where he created the social science department and the first training program for black social workers, taught sociology and economics, and developed one of the first college courses in Black Studies. In spite of the high status of these positions, neither provided financial security, alone or in tandem, and he was forced to supplement his income by teaching summer school, raising vegetables, and selling hogs and cattle.

Edmund's mother kept just as busy. She continued to work, both for pay and in a volunteer capacity, and remained actively engaged in social reform and politics. During her days at Fisk, she had learned that women like her had two areas of responsibility: the home—raising children and supporting their husbands—and work, improving the conditions of their communities. Black women of this generation were expected to work. Even those in the middle class were financially vulnerable, because education and even occupational status were rarely commensurate with income. Occupational segregation meant that black professionals were often confined to racially segregated community-based institutions and were grossly underpaid. Middle-class black families were therefore dependent on two wage earners to secure their middle-class status. They were middle class relative to other blacks but not relative to the general population.

Still, many young black women, like Rossi, extolled the virtues of women's work outside the home. Already in 1923, she was championing the rights of Negro women in the workplace and "the economic independence that will some day enable them to make their place in the ranks with other working women." Long before the women's rights movement, black female social reformers pushed for women's economic independence from men and tested the waters of gender equality. Most were themselves managing a marriage and career, and many, like Rossi, were fulfilling a third role—as mothers. Mothers to lonely little children like my father. With two parents wedded to their careers and no siblings to play with, Edmund pined for attention throughout his childhood.

The marriage may have been more practical than romantic. George and Rossi worked together and fought side by side for common causes but, as my father would later tell it, they didn't make each other happy: "My parents never separated, but maybe they should have." Years later, when poring through my grandfather's albums, I couldn't find a single photograph of Rossi. It seemed curious that a man who so meticulously archived his entire life would neglect to include such a huge piece of it. In the few pictures that I've been able to secure over the years, my grandmother wears the same high-necked, long-sleeved dress, hemline falling far below the knees, and is rarely caught smiling for the camera. The photographs embody a generation of Negro women who entered the middle class at the turn of the twentieth century. They were educated, serious churchwomen, beyond reproach by even the most rigorous standards. They tended to walk in packs of three or four. Their skirts were just a tad longer and their manners just a bit more formal. Despite Rossi's conservative attire and comportment, her views on gender equality were progressive. She admonished women to cast aside their "hang over training to shove [men] forward instead of ourselves." Yet she herself was destined to remain in the shadows of her husband.

The family took many road trips down to Letohatchee, a small town in Lowndes County, Alabama, where Rossi's mother, Big Mama, still owned the family's farm. Their first automobile—an Apperson Touring Car, nicknamed the "Jack Rabbit" for its agility and the rabbit ornament affixed to the hood—was purchased around 1917. It would have been rare to see Negroes traveling by car through the South in those days. Perhaps George's light skin and high cheekbones allowed him to skirt the color line and avoid drawing too much attention as he motored through rural Alabama. Still, he'd need to know in advance where to stop to use a restroom, get a bite to eat, or spend the night. There was, as yet, no *Negro Motorist Green Book* to guide him through the segregated South, and in Alabama, violence or the threat of violence was routinely used to keep Negroes in their place. On July 23, 1917, just days after my father's fifth birthday, brothers Jesse and William Powell were lynched in Letohatchee—a few miles from the large mulberry trees of Big Mama's farm where he passed long, listless summer days.

▼

More attention came George's way in 1918, one year after America entered the Great War. European immigration was choked by nativist forces, and four million soldiers, or doughboys, as they were then known, were dispatched overseas, opening many industrial jobs. Agents began wooing black workers to fill posts previously reserved for whites. Between 1914 and 1918, more than half a million Negroes migrated north to fill the workforce needs of the wartime economy. A new social order ignited racial and political tensions. Unionists in the industrial North resented Negroes crossing the color line, and southern planters feared losing their source of cheap labor. Protecting their constituencies, congressmen and governors across the country appealed to the federal government to stem the migration—some going as far as to suggest that blacks be restricted from crossing state lines. Meanwhile, northern employers pushed hard to expand the flow of black labor in order to meet the industrial demands of the war.

In the South, state and local ordinances were passed to impose exorbitant licensing fees on labor recruiters from the North. In some states, recruiters could even be arrested. Mailmen often confiscated newspapers they considered dangerous, such as the *Chicago Defender*, which touted the benefits of migration, posted train schedules, and declared May 15, 1917, the beginning of the "Great Northern Drive." In the summer of 1917, vicious race riots broke out in East Saint Louis, Waco, and Memphis. While reports of lynchings were ignored by President Woodrow Wilson, the mounting pressures faced by labor leaders prompted the federal government to create the Division of Negro Economics, a subcabinet of the Department of Labor. Its mission would be to mobilize black workers for the war effort and to work toward racial cooperation and opportunities for equality.

The department first considered Giles Jackson—a conservative southerner and staunch opponent of migration—to lead the division, but Du Bois lambasted him as "one of the most disreputable characters the Negro race has produced." The directors of the NAACP, the National Urban League, and the Tuskegee Institute sent a joint letter to Secretary William B. Wilson, urging him to appoint a "Negro expert on labor problems." This could have meant only one person at the time. George Haynes was the nation's leading expert on Negro migration and a champion for Negro workers' rights. With the support of Du Bois and major progressive organizations, George was appointed to head the new division, becoming the highest-ranking black federal employee at the time and the first to have any real influence at the cabinet level. Rossi worked in his shadow as assistant director, while also serving as a "dollar-a-year" worker for the Department of Labor's Women in Industry Service and a minimum-wage consultant for the domestic service section of the U.S. Employment Service.

Pop Haynes must certainly have noted the irony of advocating for racial equality and opportunity within an administration that actively sought to turn back the gains won by Negro federal workers. Under President Wilson—the first southern-born president since the Civil War—southern-style segregation was brought to the capital. Appealing to a growing white nativist sentiment—promising to end a "corrupt" Republican patronage system that had produced more than four hundred Negro federal clerks and administrators in Washington and to make the federal government more efficient (and Washington more livable)—Wilson demoted and segregated Negro federal employees, put a cap on their wages, and even barred them from eating in the cafeterias of federal buildings. And so Haynes became the highest-ranking Negro in a new racial caste system designed to limit the mobility prospects of a burgeoning black middle class.

There's a photograph of Pop Haynes that was taken during this period. He appears with the entire cabinet of the secretary of labor, the sole Negro in a sea of white men. Secretary William B. Wilson is seated in the foreground, and most of the other staff are seated around him. A few, like Pop Haynes, remain standing. There's an X suspended above his head, signifying his importance to the Haynes family. What remained undiscussed in my family was my grandfather's position in the photograph. While everyone else is spaced more or less equally apart, he stands farther apart. It's as if the men are ranked by their proximity to the secretary, their importance dwindling as they fan out around him. Pop Haynes is barely inside the room.

Despite his marginality within the department as a whole, the Division of Negro Economics had some successes. In New York, it incentivized Gimbels department store to hire Negroes, breaking the color bar in the city's retail trade. In Detroit, it encouraged the promotion of Negro workers in supervisory positions. In Pittsburgh, a local advisory committee successfully negotiated with Carnegie Steel Company to retain one-third of the Negro workers it had employed at the peak of wartime production. In Raleigh, North Carolina, it secured equal pay for Negroes performing equal work. This was an extraordinary feat for the period; not until the 1960s would America fully embrace the ideals of equal opportunity in employment for black folks.

As George penetrated the Deep South, however, he met strident opposition. With a mere government ID as his armor, he descended into this heavily segregated region, state by state, to meet with state officials and local labor leaders and to advocate for equal employment opportunities for Negroes. In other contexts, such effrontery was answered with lynchings. Throughout his journeys, he interviewed Negro sharecroppers and laborers on whether they intended to migrate to the North. One field hand encapsulated the plight of the southern Negro as follows:

Boll-weavil in de cotton,
Cut wurm in de cawn (corn)
Debil in de white man,
Wah's [war is] goin' on.

George's tenure with the division coincided with the Red Summer of 1919, one of the bloodiest periods of American racial history. With the war's end and postwar economic hardships, racial animosities resurfaced. White GIs returned home to find Negroes moving about freely in their cities. Only five years earlier, whites had had near-total hegemony in public spaces. Now, with a large and booming black presence, white mobs took to the streets to vent their frustration. A series of southern-style race riots erupted throughout the North and Midwest, and twenty-six Negro communities—including in Omaha, Tulsa, Detroit, and Washington, DC—were targeted for destruction by white mobs. Negro soldiers returning from Europe were lynched, some still wearing the uniform. In Chicago, Negroes fought back.

Just months earlier, in February 1919, Harlem's 15th New York National Guard Regiment, redesignated the 369th Infantry, had marched up Fifth Avenue and through Harlem to unprecedented cheers of hundreds of thousands of patriotic Americans. The infantry, which had fought under French command during the war, had been singled out among all American units for its courage and heroism and awarded the Croix de Guerre, France's highest military honor. Stirred by a new sense of pride, young Harlemites were drawn to the fiery rhetoric of race radicals calling for socialism, separatism, and a "new order." Harlem lyricist Andy Razaf captured the new Negro attitude in his brazen poem "The Negro Voter on Election Day":

Say Mr. Candidate, where are you from?
What of your family, from whence did they come?
What do you think of "The Birth of a Nation,"
Waco, St. Louis and race segregation?
It's all right to say you'll do this and do that—
But what have you done—let me know where I'm at?
I'm the NEW NEGRO, of much sterner stuff,
And not the "old darkey," so easy to bluff!

Although he was generally critical of black radicals and nationalists, George Haynes sometimes found himself defending them in the face of what he judged to be unfair criticism from whites. He spoke of a new "race consciousness" and cautioned that the more militant tactics of the left wing would continue to resonate with Negroes, whereas the conciliatory politics of the right (i.e., the Tuskegee school of Booker T. Washington) were increasingly being viewed as ineffective. "The time for heated debate over the so-called race problem," he declared, "is passed."

Federal support for the Division of Negro Economics began to wane in the postwar economy, and funding became strangled as early as 1919. George earned his posted salary for only a year or so and was then paid per diem and for only a few days per month. Although he appealed to remain in his post under the newly elected President William G. Harding—even without a livable salary—his appointment was terminated in 1921. (Years later, when Woodrow Wilson's legacy was examined, George Haynes, yet again, went unnoted. Even a study that focused specifically on the racial policies under Wilson—*Racism in the Nation's Service*, by Eric S. Yellin—failed to mention Haynes.)

The end of my grandfather's Washington career coincided with a new opportunity in New York. The Federal Council of Churches was just establishing a commission on race relations and was seeking a director. George—with his strong ties to the church and commitment to racial uplift—was the ideal candidate. Over the next two decades, he would use the institutional base of the church—the most powerful institution within the segregated Negro world—to push for the changes that had eluded him in the federal government. No one else, either before or since Martin Luther King, used the organizational power of the church so effectively to challenge American society to live up to his own claims of racial equality.

3

NEW NEGROES

THE Harlem that George and his family returned to in 1921 was a bustling commercial and residential district filled with black- and white-owned stores, restaurants, and houses of worship, as well as nightclubs, speakeasies, black-and-tan cabarets, and dance halls. The prevailing view at the time was that when downtown closed, uptown came to life. Looking for a space to stretch the boundaries of contemporary sexual mores, young whites, especially those with cash to burn, dressed to the nines and flocked to Harlem's valley for a walk on the wild side. Some came because they were social rebels. Others came for the music; still others as voyeurs. They came for the popular nightlife at whites-only establishments like Connie's Inn and the Cotton Club (where the patrons were all white and the performers and waiters were all black), or at Small's Paradise, where Charleston-dancing waiters carried Chinese food and bootleg liquor to an integrated clientele.

But this was only a part of Harlem. The backbone of the community was its working people: the men who worked as laborers, elevator operators, dockworkers, messengers, and porters, carrying, digging, and serving, while the women were scrubbing, cleaning, and cooking in white homes. The music,

the dancing, the laughter, masked the brutal lives they endured—
the overcrowded and overpriced tenements that they lived in
and the underpaid work that they performed.

Throughout the teens and twenties, Negroes were charged
significantly more than whites for the same Harlem properties.
This was the time of blockbusting, when real estate speculators
would buy or lease a property in Harlem and then rent it out to
blacks at a hefty profit, thus triggering a selling panic among
white residents. On January 27, 1920, the *New York Times* reported that "professional lessee" Charles Klein converted nine
apartment houses into one-room lodgings for Negroes, who paid
between $100 and $125 for units that formerly rented for $40. In
an attempt to pressure the property owners into buying out his
leases, Klein threatened to "introduce Negroes into the houses."
But the owners refused to buy Klein out, so he "advertised in the
newspapers of Newark and Baltimore for Negro tenants and
sent the clippings to the white tenants."

According to the National Urban League, which collected
demographic data on Harlemites throughout this period, Negro
families paid upward of 45 percent of their wages for housing.
The preeminent historian of Harlem, Gilbert Osofsky, refers to
the period as a "slum boom" and explains that the constant in-
flux of new migrants, combined with the restricted housing available to Negroes, led to unprecedented demand and skyrocketing
rents. Unscrupulous landlords enjoyed a windfall from fleecing
Negro tenants.

High rents and low salaries led many Harlemites to take on
boarders, sometimes strangers. This, in turn, led to congestion and
unsanitary conditions—the very makings of a slum. On October
24, 1929, the *New York Times* reported on the first annual Harlem
Health Conference and its plans to improve the living conditions
of Harlem residents. According to representatives of city health

and welfare organizations who convened the conference, "The death rate as a result of congestion . . . was 40 percent higher than the rate for the city as a whole."

Meanwhile, many companies barred blacks from any meaningful employment, and unions generally resisted black membership well into the 1930s. New York's department stores barred Negroes from employment, and even from trying on clothes. Macy's hired Negroes for only the most subservient roles, such as elevator operators, escalator attendants, and cafeteria workers, while Gimbels employed none. Even Blumstein's department store, on 125th Street—the heart of Harlem—refused to hire blacks for sales or clerical jobs. Some companies justified their discriminatory hiring practices by claiming that their white employees would object. This was, in fact, the excuse given by Metropolitan Life Insurance executives in 1930: "Not because of any prejudice on the part of the company. . . ."

The Progressive Era had been a time of contradictions for black Americans. The nation was being transformed through industrialization and capitalism, but while some Negroes were able to benefit from these changes, the solidification of the color line pushed many to the margins of society. Yet with this marginalization came an intense and unprecedented surge in literary and cultural production, especially in the big cities to which more and more black Americans migrated.

With a growing black metropolis and the dense and crisscrossing organizational networks—from churches to fraternal and benevolent associations, to burial societies, to groups like the Eastern Stars and Masons, to assorted Caribbean clubs and associations named after their home islands—Harlem became a magnet for those seeking to make it. Already, by 1912, young writers such as Countee Cullen had moved to Harlem. Others, such as Langston Hughes, Nella Larsen, Jessie Redmon Fauset, Claude McKay, and Zora Neale Hurston, soon followed, bringing a new black bohemia to Harlem.

The new Negro artist was different from the old—represented by men like Paul Laurence Dunbar, who wrote in structured, metered verse expressing muted defiance. The new guard carried a new attitude. This was a generation that came of age after slavery, and many Negro men had recently returned from fighting in World War I. Once you had a gun in your hand and a license to shoot a white man, you were no longer willing to avert your eyes or move out of the way. In his March 1925 essay for *Survey Graphic* magazine, the philosopher and critic Alain LeRoy Locke spoke of a new kind of Negro writer: "Our poets have now stopped speaking for the Negro—they speak as Negroes. Where formerly they spoke to others and tried to interpret, they now speak to their own and try to express. They have stopped posing, being nearer to the attainment of poise."

Meanwhile, my grandmother Rossi was making her own contributions to the New Negro movement, writing one of the first children's books for Negro children. At the time that it was written, the idea of instilling racial pride in black children wasn't progressive; it was radical. In games, books, and children's ditties, in postcards and advertisements, in every form of popular culture, Negro children were depicted as naked, wild, unkempt creatures with bulging white eyes and exaggerated lips. In the mid-nineteenth-century children's book *Ten Little Niggers*—in which characters' misadventures ranged from being eaten alive by alligators to burning up in the sun—children learned to count backwards by eliminating one black child at a time . . . until there were none. The first famous pickaninny in literature was

Topsy, the little slave girl in Harriet Beecher Stowe's *Uncle Tom's Cabin*. Although the 1852 novel was written as a critique of slavery, Stowe described Topsy as "one of the blackest of her race." She was "shrewd and cunning," and "there was something odd and goblin-like about her appearance—something, as Miss Ophelia afterwards said, 'so heathenish.'" As Topsy made her way from vaudeville to Broadway to the big screen—culminating in the 1927 United Artists production of *Topsy and Eva*—her humanity became barely recognizable.

With biological notions of racial differences widely argued by eminent scientists and political theorists of the day, it is no wonder that Elizabeth Ross Haynes sought to present her own child, now nearing nine years old, with a clear record of black achievement. The result was *Unsung Heroes*, a collection of biographically oriented short stories about accomplished poets, courageous leaders, and notable scientists "whom the world has failed to sing about." The book was published by W. E. B. Du Bois and Augustus Granville Dill in 1921, at the onset of the Harlem Renaissance.

Du Bois saw the construction of a new narrative for Negro children as a central task of the New Negro movement. In 1920, he launched *The Brownies' Book*, whose mission was to "make colored children realize that being 'colored' is a normal, beautiful thing." When the magazine folded a year later, he partnered with Dill, a sociologist and musician, to create Du Bois and Dill Publishers—the first black-owned press established to publish works for black children. *Unsung Heroes* was the first and only book the company published and, a decade later, Langston Hughes cited it as one of a handful of books appropriate for Negro children.

Rossi dedicated the book to her only son, Edmund. Some forty years later, he would read these very stories to my brothers and me, thrilling us with the heroic feats of Crispus Attucks, Toussaint L'Ouverture, Sojourner Truth, and Frederick Douglass. But it was Harriet Tubman and her underground railroad that held me spellbound:

> They forded rivers, climbed mountains, went through the swamps, threaded the forests with their feet sore and often bleeding. They traveled during the night and kept in hiding during the day. One of the men fell by the wayside. Harriet took out her pistol, and pointing it at his head, said, "Dead men tell no tales; you go on or die!"

▼

Although Pop had fond memories of his mother, he felt intimidated by his father. "Unless Pop Haynes volunteered information to you, you didn't dare ask him. You knew better." When visitors came, he was quickly dismissed to his room. "Children were to be seen and not heard," he bitterly recalled, "and, sometimes, not even seen." At thirteen, he was sent away to Williston Academy, an elite all-male and nearly all-white college preparatory school in Easthampton, Massachusetts. Williston boys were regarded as some of the most promising in the country and went on to top-tier colleges and universities. But, for reasons he never shared, my father returned home after just one year and enrolled in New York's Ethical Culture School. His friends were part of the elite colored bourgeoisie amassing in Harlem. (He later described Lena Horne as "one of the darker gals" in his social group.)

This was an exciting time to be young, gifted, and Negro. By 1923, Harlem was amassing a cadre of notable painters, sculptors, poets, and writers. But writers lacked access to mainstream publishing houses, and visual artists worked in almost total obscurity, with little hope of sale or access to prominent art venues. White patronage was critical to many of the most successful New Negro writers, sculptors, and painters. While some individuals, such as folklorist/writer Zora Neale Hurston, had their personal patrons (whom she dubbed "Negrotarians"), most Negro artists relied on the financial support of philanthropic institutions.

If W. E. B. Du Bois was the great agitator and visionary of the New Negro movement, George Haynes—his protégé—was its architect, forging critical partnerships and building the infrastructure to support these new artists. When Haynes returned to New York, in 1921, he headed the new Commission on Negro Churches and Race Relations, under the umbrella of the Federal Council of Churches, to foster interracial cooperation and increase contacts among the races. Key to its philosophy was the idea that negative stereotypes of Negroes could be altered through exposure to the Negro arts. The commission was the ideal base to help George build support for the movement.

He had, by now, developed an extensive network of associations, which included the retailer and philanthropist Julius Rosenwald and the real estate magnate and philanthropist William E. Harmon. He worked with Harmon to establish the Harmon Foundation Awards, which gave out generous cash prizes in the areas of literature, music, fine arts, business, science, religion, education, and race relations. George was selected to administer the awards, putting him in close contact with the most renowned African-American writers and artists of the era. The list of recipients amounted to a virtual who's who of the Harlem Renaissance: Aaron Douglas, Laura Wheeler Waring, Palmer Hayden, Archibald Motley, James Weldon Johnson, Langston Hughes, Claude McKay, Florence Mills, and Countee Cullen. In 1926, after receiving the first gold medal award in literature for his very first volume of poetry, *Color*, Cullen sent George a

handwritten note, thanking him for the $400, "for which, be-
longing to the indigent profession which claims me, I shall have
small trouble in making use."

▼

Although the Harlem Renaissance has often been characterized
as a time when whites partook of black culture, relations between whites and blacks were multifaceted. Appropriation and
mimicry, along with a cross-fertilization of political ideas and
cultural motifs, fueled the production of art during the Roar-
ing Twenties. The 1921 novel *Birthright*—written by the white
Tennessee writer T. S. Stribling—was embraced by both blacks
and whites. The *New York Tribune* heralded it as the best southern novel in a decade, and Harlem Renaissance writers Jessie
Fauset, Nella Larsen, and Walter White cited it as their inspiration to create truer portraits of black life. Bolstered by his first
success, Stribling set out to build a trilogy, and he turned to his
friend George Haynes for guidance on "the better side of Negro
life." (The two men had already formed a business partnership
and were investing in real estate in both Harlem and Brooklyn.)
Confident that Stribling could alter white perceptions of Negroes, Haynes provided him with a bibliography of books on
Negro life as well as a list of towns that he should visit, in both
the rural South and the urban North. The book that grew out of
this research, *The Store*, later won the Pulitzer Prize.

By the time my grandparents purchased the property at 411
Convent Avenue, George had amassed a fair amount of capital
from his real estate ventures. In addition to his partnership with
Stribling, he had formed his own investment company and ac-
quired several properties in Harlem's fashionable Heights. It
was 1931, and the nation was just beginning to spiral into the
Depression. The purchase was surely a great bargain.

411 Convent Avenue was a grand home. The entryways to each room were built of thick mahogany. Tiled fireplaces with five-foot-tall mahogany mantelpieces and built-in mirrors graced each room on the first floor, where visitors were entertained. A formal parlor, sealed off by double doors, was likely the spot where my grandfather received his friend and longtime mentor W. E. B. Du Bois. Ceiling-high pocket doors opened to the music room, where a baby grand piano, polished with bowling alley wax, dominated the space. A third room—a formal dining room—was flanked by six-foot-high wood panels. The house would have still been in its prime in the early 1930s. The oak floors were hand-waxed. The walls were freshly painted. The glass doors sparkled and the brass knobs shined.

During Du Bois's visits, the two men would certainly have discussed the nine black boys in Alabama who, in 1931, had been wrongfully convicted of rape. Known as the Scottsboro Boys, their case had galvanized radicals, liberals, and moderates across the nation and had become an international cause célèbre, thanks in part to the American Communist Party and its legal arm, the International Labor Defense (ILD). Despite the party's success in bringing international attention to the case, building interracial alliances, and linking black protest to a universal struggle against injustice, many black mainstream organizations, including the NAACP, were skeptical of its motives. In 1934, a group of Harlem businessmen, newspaper editors, and ministers, along with the defendants' attorney, Samuel Leibowitz, formed the American Scottsboro Committee. Its goal was to mount an aggressive public relations campaign to wrest control from the Communist Party while also building financial support for the legal defense team. They asked George Haynes—now race relations secretary of the Federal Council of Churches—to serve as its chair. The committee had only limited success; several of the defendants, along with their parents, remained loyal to the ILD, crediting it as the "sole organization in the country that has kept the Scottsboro disgrace before the world." In 1935, when the Supreme Court agreed to hear the case, George's committee would need to coordinate with the ILD, working out which entity would represent which defendant. Although this divvying up of responsibilities fell short of the full-scale collaboration that the ILD had hoped for, it nonetheless established the Communist Party as a force in black politics.

The conversations between Haynes and Du Bois likely reflected the diverging paths their lives were taking. Haynes remained committed to the promise of racial equality through Christian brotherhood. He used his base at the church to appeal for justice for all of America's oppressed—Negroes, Native Americans, Asians, and Mexicans. The more senior Du Bois was beginning to question whether racial equality in America was even possible. By 1934, he had become immersed in Marxist political thought and was advocating "volunteer segregation" and black economic cooperatives.

My grandfather would surely have been ill at ease with Du Bois's radicalism; he had spent his life fighting for racial integration and eschewed the politics of socialism, which he saw as a rejection of America. Yet he also defied political pigeonholing; in the 1920s, he had declared full support for the Pan-African Congress—a group of progressive African, Afro-American, and Afro-Caribbean intellectuals and leaders who demanded self-determination for colonial subjects and championed reforms for blacks throughout the African diaspora. And although he founded the largest bootstrap self-help organization for blacks in the nation (the National Urban League), he also agitated for inclusion in the newly evolving social welfare apparatus of the 1930s. Haynes understood that as the federal government restructured the national economy through the New Deal programs of the 1930s—the Public Works Administration, the Tennessee Valley Authority, the National Industrial Recovery Act, the

Agricultural Adjustment Act, and the Social Security Act—most Negro Americans stood little to gain without special protection clauses. He used the influential black publication the *Chicago Defender* to make his case, appealing to "intelligent Negroes all over the country" to "write and telegraph their Congressmen, Senators and the President urging that such provisions be included in all security laws."

The two men's political visions played out against the politics, protests, and early civil rights victories of the Depression era. Adam Clayton Powell Jr. was rising to power in Harlem, organizing rent strikes, boycotts, and picket lines and integrating the workforce at Harlem Hospital, the New York City Transit Authority, and the utility companies. In 1935, Harlem's first riot occurred, triggered by rumors that a young Puerto Rican accused of shoplifting had been killed by police officers. In 1937, Asa Philip Randolph negotiated the first contract for a black union—the Brotherhood of Sleeping Car Porters—and Joe Louis (the Brown Bomber) became the heavyweight boxing champion of the world. One year earlier, Jesse Owens had won four gold medals at the 1936 Olympics held in Nazi Germany. For the first time, white Americans embraced blacks as true American heroes.

Over the next two decades, Du Bois and Haynes would remain close friends. Even as my grandfather approached his eighties (and Du Bois, his nineties), he continued to seek his mentor's feedback and expressed his love and admiration. The two men and their wives would entertain one another well into the 1950s—the Du Boises in their Brooklyn home on Grace Court, the Hayneses (now with a new Mrs. Haynes) in Mount Vernon.

❧

Pop didn't leave home again until 1934, when he began his undergraduate studies at Wilberforce University, in Ohio, the oldest

black private university in the country. This was another chapter
of his life that he kept guarded. He never mentioned any college
friends or groups that he belonged to. In fact, he seems like a
ghost in his own college yearbook. Of the one hundred twenty
seniors in the graduating class of 1938—most of whom cite dozens
of activities and affiliations, including religious and secular clubs,
political organizations, sororities and fraternities, sports, and
choir—he alone lists a single entry: Social Administration (Ass't).
He is one of the few graduates to give no forwarding address in
the senior class directory. He appears in neither the class history
of 1938 nor the prophecy of the senior class. Nor the class horo-
scope. At least at Wilberforce, my father had no history and no
future. In his graduation picture, he wears the customary suit
and tie but strikes a deadpan gaze off to the right. Next to his
picture is a simple quote, later made famous by Bob Marley:
"Wake up and live." He apparently did, indeed, once he left
Wilberforce, as attested to by the countless photographs with
different women that I later unearthed. Along with the photos
were two divorce documents, each issued within a year of each
other. Both marriages had begun and ended during the war
and lasted barely a year. No formal ceremonies were held. No
progeny were issued. In fact, his marriages cost him little more
than the lawyer fees to end them.

Pop was stationed in Okinawa during the war and, like many
Negroes in the segregated army, was relegated to peripheral
duties. He served in the 260th Quartermaster Corps as a clerk
typist. Although nearly one million Negro GIs fought in the war,
most did not serve in combat or fly planes. (One notable exception is the Buffalo Soldiers—the more than thirteen thousand
Negro soldiers who fought in Italy during World War II and
won more than twelve thousand decorations and citations for
their bravery). The vast majority of Negroes who served in the

war cleared roads of mines, built airfields, loaded and unloaded cargo (which often included bombs and explosives), and drove the trucks that serviced the fighting units. Luckily, Pop's typing skills kept him in an office.

Not only was the U.S. Army racially segregated at home and abroad, but so too was the entire industrial apparatus supporting the war effort. More than a quarter of a million defense jobs were closed to black workers. In the aircraft industry alone, only 240 of the 107,000 workers were black. This was probably the first time Pop had come face to face with the kind of overt segregation that Negroes of lesser means regularly faced. Later, he would boast to us about sneaking into the white side of the barrack to watch movies, his light skin providing cover in the twilight hours.

The early 1940s was the height of the black left in America and the period when coalition building among longtime rivals reached its organizational peak. Segregation had steered black folks to turn inward, giving rise to new cultural forms and mobilizing black communities across political spectrums. Communists, socialists, and nationalists worked alongside the National Negro Congress, the NAACP, and the National Urban League to dismantle Jim Crow segregation. They marched together, attended joint rallies, and petitioned companies like Sperry Gyroscope, in Long Island, which produced computer-controlled stabilizers and airborne radar equipment for bombs and airplanes, to desegregate the workplace. In 1941, A. Philip Randolph, a socialist and the international president of the Brotherhood of Sleeping Car Porters, threatened a march on Washington to protest racial discrimination and segregation in the armed forces and military industries. It was, in fact, the threat of thousands of Negroes marching on Washington that prompted Franklin Roosevelt to sign Executive Order 8802, banning racial discrimination in national defense contracts. For the first time, blacks gained access to industrial jobs, so that, in 1943, my mother could take a job as a telegraph operator—a job previously barred to Negro workers.

My father was never a man to take risks. After the war, he enrolled at the Atlanta School of Social Work, one of a handful of schools producing Negro social workers. This would be the first of many compromises he would make. He had dreamed of becoming an engineer but was convinced that he'd be over-reaching as a black man. Although the GI Bill made it possible for many veterans to enter science and engineering programs, most universities were still highly segregated. Even proponents of desegregation described black Americans as "ill-prepared not just educationally, but psychologically and even morally, for scientific careers." Still, MIT accepted Negroes during the 1930s and 1940s, and black institutions like Howard University and a few land-grant schools regularly graduated black engineers. But Pop lacked the gumption of his father, and perhaps the mathematical chops he'd need to compete, so he took the road more traveled, joining the growing ranks of black professional social workers in the country. Social work was becoming a part of the new employment wave that could secure a middle-class lifestyle while still supporting old-time community values.

Prior to the 1940s, black social workers were a rare breed. Among the 135,964 black professionals and semiprofessionals in 1930—representing a mere 2.1% of all black workers—nearly half were teachers. In fact, classroom teachers, music teachers, and clergymen accounted for two-thirds of the Negro professional class. Dentists, lawyers, judges, and physicians accounted for another 5 percent. Together, they represented the Talented Tenth, a Negro leadership class largely composed of light-skinned Negroes. It was rare to see dark-skinned girls like Daisy Delphine

Alexander—the woman who would become Ed's third wife—in university graduate programs.

Daisy was a sassy southern girl from Rocky Mount, North Carolina, a classic Carolina town split by race and railroad tracks. She had been raised by her beautician mother and her schoolteacher aunt in a small house on Atlantic Avenue, just down the street from the tobacco fields and a world away from the New England private schools and black renaissance of my father's childhood. The great granddaughter of a Negro slave and a Tuscarora Indian who had been kidnapped into slavery as a young girl, Daisy was an arresting beauty. She was petite, with rich, dark skin and long, straight black hair that would have displayed her Tuscarora roots had she not kept it short and permed.

Though her roots were rural and humble, the women in her family were educated. Her grandmother, Millicent Ann Smith—born in Smithfield, North Carolina, in 1872—had been one of the first graduates of Shaw University, the first college established for Negroes in the South. Like other early Negro colleges, it had been founded by the American Baptist Home Mission Society to provide Christian instruction to emancipated slaves. A pillar of the community, Millie had also been a member of the Order of the Eastern Star (the women's auxiliary to the Prince Hall Freemasons) and a founder of the Saint James Baptist Church. She married William Alexander Frazier—a cook for the Jefferson Hotel in Richmond, Virginia, and a messenger for the Atlantic Coast Line Railroad. (Mom always said that we were related to E. Franklin Frazier, the most famous Negro sociologist of the era.) Together they had thirteen children, eight of whom died in infancy. Among the five to survive was Daisy's mother, Mattie Frazier, who also attended Shaw University, studying with the school's founder and president, Dr. Henry Martin Tupper.

When it was Daisy's turn to attend college, Mattie put her on a train for Greensboro, North Carolina, where Bennett College was located, and warned her to remain in her compartment for the 135-mile journey. This was sound advice for a seventeen-year-old colored girl, who, in the 1940s Jim Crow South, had few rights that any white man was required to respect. Bennett had only recently become a women's college, and it drew daughters from the most distinguished families, many of whom were of mixed European ancestry and thus were light-skinned, with "good hair"—that is, long, straight hair. Daisy was one of the brownest gals at Bennett, but she used her charm to break into the right social circles and circumvent the "brown bag test"—those whose skin was darker than a brown paper bag were generally excluded from status-conscious groups like the Alpha Kappa Alpha sorority.

When Daisy graduated, in 1943, there were only a few professional paths open to black women: teaching, nursing, and social work. The last was directly tied to community building and racial uplift. Most social workers were still untrained, and only a few graduate programs in the South were available to Negroes. Daisy never even bothered to apply to Howard University, still known for not accepting dark-skinned blacks. She settled instead on Atlanta University, which held the oldest and most prestigious social work program in the nation, save for the few Negro slots at Columbia and Chicago.

She was all of five foot one in heels and twenty-one years old when she started graduate school. Ed was thirty-one and resembled a young Denzel Washington. Tall and slim, a thin mustache over his upper lip, light-skinned and a little cocky, he was accustomed to women swooning and fawning over him. But he had never come across a proud, self-assured woman like Daisy, who swooned for no man and expected to be courted like a proper Southern belle. She favored pearls for formal wear but, for the everyday, she wore silk blouses with a little diamond stud or gold pin clipped to her jacket vest pocket. Her eyebrows were lightly plucked, her nails long and perfectly manicured, and she had already adopted much of her signature look: blood-red lipstick and high heels.

They met on the bus one spring afternoon in 1944; he fell hard and proposed marriage within months. Whether Ed ever intended to bring up his previous marriages or their significance simply waned with each passing day, his past remained buried for some twenty years. Nor did the subject of color come up, despite the fact that "marrying dark" was frowned upon by the more self-conscious of the Talented Tenth. Pop Haynes, who had long embraced Africa and all things black, welcomed Daisy with open arms.

The war had ushered in a new prosperity, and Negroes were enjoying the largest jump in earnings since emancipation. It was in this postwar euphoria that newlyweds Ed and Daisy Haynes moved into the large limestone at 411 Convent Avenue. It was a coming home for Ed and a rise to bourgeois respectability for Daisy. Yet the house, now vacated by Pop Haynes, was not a wedding gift, as Ed had hoped. In fact, he would never get over the fact that he had to buy his childhood home from his father, who had moved north to Mount Vernon even as Ed's mother was left behind. Like everything else in our family, the abandonment of my grandmother—after thirty-five years of marriage—was never discussed. We never learned whether Pop Haynes had left her for another woman, whether they had battled for more than common causes, or whether they had simply grown apart. She remained in our home for the next five years, until her death, in 1953. Du Bois and his wife, Shirley Graham, sent a letter of condolence to Pop Haynes at his Mount Vernon address, remembering Elizabeth for her insight and courage. Two years later, they wrote again to congratulate him on his marriage

to Olyve Love Jeter, the noted classical pianist and Haynes's longtime secretary.

⬥

By 1950, New York's black population had grown to more than
seven hundred thousand, and the vast majority lived in Harlem.
Over the next decade, Central Harlem would become an entrenched ghetto. Although most residents were employed, labor
was highly segregated, as was the urban housing market. Federal
policy shifted resources out of the cities and into the construction of highways to the suburbs. Whites soon followed, fleeing
the hordes of new black migrants and the growing numbers of
Puerto Ricans who had begun settling East Harlem.

Daisy and Ed maintained a proper middle-class home in
Sugar Hill (which was still somewhat sheltered from the corro-
sion of the valley) and were socially active with other black professionals in and out of Harlem—lawyers, doctors, teachers, and
fellow social workers. They entertained frequently and took nu-
merous photographs of themselves standing outside 411 Convent
Avenue, Daisy smiling, waving, sometimes in a mink coat, other
times in a sundress that displayed her fine figure.

My two brothers—George III and Alan Ross (named for our
grandmother Rossi)—were born within the first four years of
my parents' marriage. Both were given piano lessons and attended the progressive Mayfair Nursery School on 143rd Street.
(George's nursery school certificate, dated June 26, 1955, was
signed by Beatrice Canegata Mayfield, the stepmother of famed
boxer, actor, and civil rights trailblazer Canada Lee.) They each
had their own playroom on the third floor, filled with the latest
toys from FAO Schwarz and Polk's Model Craft Hobbies. They
attended Jack and Jill and Hansel and Gretel, the black social
clubs that ensured one's children would meet the right kind of

playmate from the right family. (Later, George even attended a few black cotillions, where the fathers of the young debutantes were introduced as admirals and captains—exactly the kind of behavior that exemplified the pretentiousness and frivolities of the black middle class that sociologist E. Franklin Frazier had railed against.) Every Christmas, right up to the year I was born, the two boys were dressed in bow ties and jackets to be photographed for the annual holiday postcards, quite popular during the era.

Our grandfather died in 1960, ten months before I was born. He left generous inheritances to both George and Alan. Although Pop inherited a number of properties, the only personal possession left to him was a pocket watch—yet another slight that he would grumble about for years to come. I often wonder whether Pop would have been more forgiving toward his father had history remembered George Haynes differently. Perhaps he would have come to look back more fondly on the absent father and to justify the lack of closeness between them. Perhaps he could have leveraged the family history, had that history been more celebrated. But, by the end of my grandfather's life, few remembered George Haynes. Even the National Urban League seemed to have forgotten him and largely dismissed the family. I, in turn, grew up with the vague vanity of knowing I had an important grandfather that nobody had ever heard of. And Pop was left with the dying social networks of a generation past.

Later, Pop would vacillate between striving toward and shying away from the world of his father. He talked for years about getting into politics, as his father had always urged him to do, but he pursued it in fits and starts. By the time he gathered up the muster to throw his hat in the ring, in the early 1980s—for deputy commissioner of parole—it was too late. He had no political backing. All of his father's friends and connections were long gone, and nobody knew who Ed Haynes was. The National

Urban League was aware of his presence, but he felt snubbed and dismissed by the organization, another chip for his heavy shoulders. He had joined 100 Black Men of America—the civic organization for professional black men—but he wasn't one to schmooze or work the room. And then there was the back-scratching, the political favors, and the inevitable corruption that he loathed. Our mother called it a false sense of ethics, that he was so honest he was stupid. After his short and spectacularly unsuccessful run for deputy commissioner, he gave up politics for good.

Given his impressive family background and the distinguished schools he attended, you could say my father was an underachiever. He had dreamed of becoming an engineer but settled for a career in social work. His first job after graduate school, and one he would hold for his entire career, was as a parole officer in the New York State Division of Parole in the Bronx. He was among a handful of blacks in his unit and one of the few officers, black or white, with a master's degree. He carried an elite status in a small and stifling world.

4

SOUL DOLLARS

A s a youngster, I came to know Harlem as a sprawling group of contiguous neighborhoods above 110th Street. What looked to outsiders like one giant black belt was actually subdivided into many distinct areas: Manhattanville, Morningside Heights, Mount Morris Park, Central Harlem (the valley), West Harlem, and Spanish Harlem (known locally as El Barrio or East Harlem). Our own neighborhood—the area around City College—was officially known as Hamilton Heights and, unofficially, as Sugar Hill.

In the 1960s, the stretch of 125th Street from the Harlem River to Fifth Avenue was the epicenter of soul, a term that conveyed both the essence of being black and a newfound sense of self-determination. Alan and George—seven and ten years my seniors—often let me tag along with them on trips down to the valley, where soul brothers, soul food, and soul power were all on display. We stopped at Bobby's Happy House and the Harlem Record Shack to hear the latest soul hits, and at the National Memorial African Bookstore, also known as "The House of Common Sense and the Home of Proper Propaganda."

Outside the bookstore, streetcorner preachers vied for space with proselytizers from the Nation of Islam.

"As-salaam alaikum, my young brother. Can I interest you in a *Mohammed Speaks?* No? How 'bout a bean pie?"

"You! You! Black man! You think that's your woman, but let you go out of town and go see what happens!"

"Excuse me, my beautiful sister. Can I offer you some education?"

The new black attitude rejected the processed hair popular among the bourgeoisie and embraced a natural aesthetic. By the late 1960s, black was beautiful and Afros were everywhere. More importantly, my brother Alan had grown a huge bushy Afro. I copied most everything he did, and by age six I was letting my hair grow out, too.

Within a few years my "shape-up" had become too long for the old-time neighborhood barbers, many of whom never learned how to properly cut a 'fro. So, rather than wait in the long lines outside Jerry's Den on 125th Street, I started accompanying my mother to Raymond's Beauty Shop on Saint Nicholas Avenue to get a proper blowout—meaning the hair was cut, washed, dried under a flip-top hair dryer, and then, while still slightly damp, picked out with a wide-tooth comb, leaving a fluffier, bushier head of hair.

Daisy had her hair styled in a bouffant—an elaborate beehive updo, complete with fringed bangs—which was popular among the more glamour-conscious women. Sometimes she wore her hair down and accentuated the look with extensions. Unlike Grandma Mattie's storefront beauty shop in Montclair, New Jersey, which catered to old church ladies and reeked of fried hair and Murray's Pomade, Raymond's carried the distinct scent of sweet coconut hairspray and Ultra Sheen, the vibe of a sophisticated salon.

Harlem beauty parlors served as a hub for a thriving underground economy. Numbers runners made their rounds for the "policy racket"—the poor man's lottery—taking down bets that stood to make a six-to-one return. Street hustlers stopped by regularly, selling their wares—anything from designer dresses and handbags to steaks and shoes, all to be had for a song.

Some parlors allowed hustlers to temporarily set up shop in the corner. More frequently, they worked the room. Each hustler had his own style. Some would walk halfway down the aisle, drop their bags to the floor, and deliver their pitch. "I've got Chanel Number Five, ladies. Fifteen dollars. Two for twenty." Others took a more personal approach, removing just a few sample items from supersized shopping bags and zigzagging the room while engaging in friendly banter.

"Ladies, I have some beautiful silk blouses today. Short sleeves, long sleeves, three-quarter sleeves. Sleek and soft! Sleek and soft! Just like you, sweetheart!"

They'd invariably single out one or two women ("This one's your color!"), holding the blouse up against them. "Now *that* is your color! You can't tell me that doesn't look fine!"

The meat man traveled by car and brought in boxes of prepackaged, unlabeled steaks. Striding through the shop, a few steaks balanced carefully on his arm, he'd search out the crowd for the least sign of interest and then pass his arm under a prospect's nose. "Prime filet mignon. Big and juicy, ain't it, baby? No? Say, how about you, brother? Best deal in Harlem!"

Daisy often came home with a new hairdo and a stack of filets mignons, setting off yet another argument with Pop—Mr. Law Enforcement. Taking paper clips from the office was "stealing" in his book; buying filet mignon "off the back of a truck" at the beauty parlor was too much for him to bear.

Raymond's Beauty Shop drew a wide assortment of colorful characters, starting with Raymond, its owner. Before the word *disco* became popularized or Patti LaBelle put on a gold and silver lamé spacesuit, Raymond would dazzle the denizens in his nighttime attire. In the photographs he hung up or passed around at his shop, he looked as much the diva as Patti ever did, dressed in three-inch platform shoes, silver lamé cape, and thick makeup. But Disco Raymond only came out at night. By day, he played the role of a Harlem ladies' man. His nails were manicured and he wore Italian shoes and hip-hugging dress slacks under his apron. He had strong looks, trim sideburns, and an athletic build. He was charismatic, could carry a tune, and drew the attentions of men and women alike. (When he began shedding pounds in the late 1970s, no one understood what was happening. But, in June 1981, when the first medical report on a new immunodeficiency disease came out, many of us in the neighborhood thought about Raymond.)

The guy who cut my hair, Joe, was a hulk of a man who might have passed for a halfback if it had not been for his demonstrative gestures and feminine lilt. It was a bit unsettling to be preened and fussed over by Joe as he exchanged catty gossip with the female staff: how Delilah wasn't fooling anyone with those extensions or so and so had no business wearing hot pants. I enjoyed the touch of his hands as he massaged my scalp and stroked my head, and I wondered whether that made me a sissy. Pop was intolerant of anything he deemed sissy. "You'll be a sissy if you put that polish on your nails," he'd warn me. What did I know about these boundaries between men and women? I saw hipsters and hustlers at the beauty parlor having their nails trimmed and buffed right beside me. They didn't seem to be sissies. I thought a clear coat made me look like Super Fly, and Mom didn't mind lending me her polish.

Gender benders were a part of the Harlem landscape of my childhood. One woman who frequented Raymond's smoked a stogie and wore a men's suit and tie. No one gave her a second look. In this space where men performed like women, she stood out and blended in all at once. Another neighborhood character, Chris, ran the corner newsstand at 148th and Saint Nicholas.

Chris was a woman stuck in a man's body. She wore dresses and heels; her hair was long and always seemed to be at various stages of losing its perm. As a child, I was struck by the combination of perfect cleavage and the five o'clock shadow that often seeped through her heavy makeup.

The idea that black gay men were stuck in the closet like their counterparts downtown does not fully capture the picture of 1960s Harlem, where drag queens found outlets as "female impersonators" on stage at the Apollo, pimps dressed in mink and rabbit, womanizers were so meticulous in their grooming and preoccupied with their image that they were indistinguishable from gay men, and charisma and flamboyance went hand in hand. Everybody knew somebody in their church who was a little too effeminate, who might cause them to wonder if brother so and so "swings that way." But in a community that was desperate for resources, men who had talent and energy and know-how were not easily dismissed.

Harlem was full of contradictions for anyone who dared to look. Mamie Canty, my mother's seamstress, was also a full-time bookie for Harlem kingpin Nicky Barnes, one of the biggest drug dealers in the city. I often accompanied my mother to Mamie's home, down on Adam Clayton Powell Jr. Boulevard, near Central Park North, to have a dress altered or to shop for designer dresses, suits, and colognes, which Mamie always seemed to come by mysteriously and to part with at outrageously low prices. Tall, thin, and dark-skinned, she had a droopy eye, likely the result of a stroke. She was also a bit wobbly on her feet, as if suffering from a longtime ailment. But she exuded style and sophistication. I usually waited in her bedroom, with its king-size bed and large TV console—always on and muted—while my mother and Mamie talked business in the living room. Sometimes a rack of clothes, uncannily similar to the ones in the downtown department stores, stretched across her bed. Jazz

from the 1940s—Cab Calloway, Mildred Bailey, Charlie Parker—
played in the background.

Everything Mamie owned—clothing, furnishings, art—was
select and expensive. Once, she sold us a six-foot marble table, a
one-of-a-kind piece that even back then must have been valued
at several thousand dollars. In Harlem, where every barber or
beauty salon accommodated a piece of the underground economy, Mamie's high-end offerings didn't seem unusual. Years
later, Daisy would be stunned to read in the local papers that
Mamie had been arrested for drug trafficking. The ring, headquartered at her house, controlled the heroin sold on 111th and
112th Streets, between Lenox and Eighth Avenues. By then,
Mamie's beautiful marble table had long-since lost its sheen.
Water spots and rust stains had accumulated from the tin pans
and water glasses that my father had deployed over the years to
improvise a home humidifier system.

In Harlem, if it wasn't off the books, it was likely overpriced.
Residents, regardless of class, were overcharged and underserved
for the most basic of necessities. For years, the major super-
market chains steered clear of black neighborhoods and the locally owned shops offered neither variety nor quality. Most folks
in our neighborhood shopped at the Food Family, at 147th Street
and Saint Nicholas Avenue, which was owned by two short,
balding, well-fed brothers. They were ethnic in that inimitable
way that only a New York shopkeeper can be—tough-talking,
street-savvy, nobody's-fool ethnic. They wore big gold watches
and thick gold chains with a large dangling cross prominently
displayed, along with their chest hairs. With their sleeves rolled
up and their shirts buttoned down, a cigar hanging out the side
of the mouth, they exuded split-second savvy. They watched the
customers like hawks, never sure who was there to buy and who
was there to steal, and they would chase a teenager down the
block over a package of hamburger meat. But they could be

friendly and charming, especially with Daisy, who always got a deal. The problem was that, as in many food stores in Harlem, the meat was old (and injected with water for added weight), the milk spoiled within a few days of purchase, the scales were loaded, and the prices were inflated.

Food Family had narrow aisles and miniature shopping carts. At the front of the store, less than four feet from the cashier, a single line of chrome railings separated two different economies. Fifteen-year-old boys waited on the other side, calling out their services to single or elderly women. "Hey, miss! Would you like some help with your groceries?" Before the women had time to answer, the boys leaped over the railing and started bagging their items. This act was a show of good faith, an enticement thrown in for free. The real service they were selling was lugging grocery bags across city blocks for overburdened moms and grandmas. The added bonus was protection; walking down Harlem's streets with shopping bags could be dangerous, especially for a woman. It targeted you as someone who was likely carrying cash. For a small tip, the boys would carry the bags for the women, ensuring that they and their groceries arrived home safely.

For years, I was in awe of these big boys. They seemed so independent and confident, and they were making serious money— at least by my standards. Both Alan and George had worked stints as bag boys at the Food Family, and I was determined to follow, once I grew old enough. But by the time I reached adolescence, the Food Family had become a steady hangout for seedy neighborhood characters. Batteries were locked in glass cases and guards took the place of bag boys outside the railing.

Barbara, the checkout girl, never failed to catch my eye. She was tall and slim, with striking brown eyes that were accentuated by fake eyelashes, looking too glamorous for a checkout girl. Yet as she manned the checkout counter year after year, the sparkle in her eyes faded a little bit more and her gaze drifted farther off as she picked up each item, punched the bulky keys, and hit the Return button on the old mechanical cash register. She was trapped, with no prospects of anything better. Jobs such as hers once served as a second source of income, but with the increasing underemployment of black men, they now provided what an entire family had to live on. With rent and the price of food inflated, the working poor had to run even faster just to stay in place. They were desperate targets for payday lenders, who charged up to 400 percent interest on short-term cash loans, or for rent-to-own outlets, where customers with poor credit paid double the cost over the life of a lease. What sociologist David Caplovitz discovered in his 1967 study, hailed as a landmark at the time, was not breaking news for folks like Barbara: the poor pay more.

Most of the services in Harlem were subpar, and its schools were no exception. As the bulk of postwar prosperity continued to flow out to the suburbs, blacks, Hispanics, and new immigrants of color flowed into the inner city. Residential segregation led to educational segregation. By 1964, most black children in New York attended schools that were over 90 percent nonwhite. These schools had few experienced teachers and were burdened with large class sizes—sometimes as many as fifty-five students in a class. Once a teacher accumulated five years of teaching, he or she was guaranteed, under a deal struck between the city and the teachers union, the right to transfer, further undermining the ability of inner-city schools to amass a strong teaching force. Incentives to attract experienced teachers to black schools— known as "combat pay"—were largely unsuccessful. Black children in the city fell further behind, reading, on average, two grade levels below their white counterparts.

At my own neighborhood school—P.S. 186, at 145th Street, between Broadway and Amsterdam Avenues—the kids reflected the full diversity of the catchment area. They came from the tree-lined avenues of Convent and Saint Nicholas Terrace, the commercial strips along Broadway, Amsterdam, and Saint Nicholas, and pockets of poverty within the stretch of 142nd and 152nd Streets, between Amsterdam and Broadway. They lived in brownstones, apartment buildings, walk-ups, and run-down tenements. As in many New York public schools, classrooms were overcrowded. There were thirty-six kids in my first- and second-grade classes, and some of them were pretty tough.

I learned in school that it wasn't good to be too dark or too light in the black community. It was hard to sort out, though. While light skin could be a status marker, "high yellow" could be an insult. Kids would fight over being called jet black, yet soul was *in* and black was supposedly beautiful. I had always thought of myself as dark, but when I started school I saw that there were many kids a lot darker than me. No one made fun of me for my skin color; I was picked on because I was short and skinny. I was always the smallest kid in the class, at the front of every line, and so size became my preoccupation. I was determined to prove that I was tough, even if it meant getting hurt. I still have a two-and-a-half-inch scar on my knee from my fight with Tyrone, the biggest and most unruly kid in the class. Many a yardstick had been broken over his butt, despite the fact that corporal punishment had been banned in New York public schools for decades.

One day, Tyrone grabbed my Russian Cossack hat, hoping to engage me in a chase around the schoolyard. My mother had bought the hat downtown, where it was the latest in men's fashion—perfect for attending a Broadway play or shopping at Saks Fifth Avenue. But at P.S. 186 it made me stand out like a sore thumb, when all I wanted was to fit in.

I chased Tyrone furiously as he dodged around the other children, and even after I came crashing down on the cement, busting my knee wide open, he continued to laugh, falling to the ground in hysteria. Boiling with anger, I got up and kicked him in the gut. Now we were both crying. That night, Pop took a big bottle of iodine and had my brothers hold me down while he poured it into the gash, because he was too cheap to take me to the emergency room.

We all knew our ranks, and by the final months of second grade I had graduated to being the third-toughest kid in my class. But before I could complete the school year, the entire public school system threatened to topple. The mantra of community control had been reverberating throughout the city, as parents and local activists staged sit-ins at the board of education and indicted the New York public school system as a racist conspiracy to deny the children of the ghetto an education. The city worked hard to defuse tensions and, in spring 1967, established three experimental community schools throughout New York: Intermediate School 201, in East Harlem; Ocean Hill–Brownsville, in Brooklyn; and a third school on the Lower East Side of Manhattan.

Mayor John Lindsay and community activists were supportive of the plan, but the largely white and heavily Jewish union feared that the newly empowered schools would undermine job security, collective bargaining power, and due process. Indeed, within one year, the new board at Ocean Hill–Brownsville abruptly fired thirteen teachers, along with six administrators. The incident pitted the New Left against organized labor, and united Catholics and Jews against blacks. That next fall, the United Federation of Teachers and the Council of School Supervisors & Administrators went on a series of strikes against the community control of schools. With almost 90 percent of the city's teachers and administrators honoring picket lines, the

SOUL DOLLARS ▐ 75

New York City school system was virtually shut down for much
of the fall. More than a million public school students were
affected. But I would not be one of them.

Conditions at P.S. 186 had been on the decline for years, and
my parents were becoming increasingly concerned about my
education and safety. The last straw came in the spring of second
grade, when I was mugged in the boys' washroom by a fifth grader
(the boy stole my Hopalong Cassidy watch). That summer, my
parents rushed to find a private school that would accept me on
short notice. Drawing on her endless Rolodex of personal associations, my mother placed a call to Allonia Gadsden, the black
director of the private, progressive Emerson School downtown
and an adviser to the Children's Television Workshop. Just like
that, I was enrolled in third grade for the fall. "You pays your
money, you takes your choice," Daisy said.

The switch would make all the difference. A decade later, my
old second-grade pal Michael (a short, stocky kid with loads
of heart and charisma) would greet me from his corner on the
block, where he was now dealing drugs, patting me on my back
and telling me that he was proud of me. By that time, P.S. 186
was gone; its conditions had deteriorated to the point where the
city had shut it down. In another thirty years, trees were growing out of the building, pigeons flew through open windows,
and drug dealers brought new rules to the small classrooms.

Our street was already changing by the late 1960s. A few
limestones, including the one next to ours, had already been converted to rooming houses. Another sign of change was the stealing of trashcans—the thirty-two-gallon metal ones—and their
lids. Residents started chaining them to their stoops and spray-
painting their addresses on the lids and cans. And they began
locking the outside doors to block access to their hallway vesti-
bules, which were becoming a popular hangout for the growing
number of heroin addicts. The double doors to our own house

were padlocked to an anchor in the vestibule floor. To further deter would-be muggers, my father installed three sets of locks on the front door.

I had witnessed my first mugging when I was five. Mrs. Grandberry was walking me to kindergarten class one morning. About twenty paces ahead of us, a heavyset woman was turning up 147th Street toward Amsterdam Avenue when a young man who'd been concealed in the entryway of a garden apartment darted out and grabbed her purse. She toppled backwards and landed on the pavement. Her stockings were torn and her hands were scraped from catching herself on the cement. She was crying as we helped her to her feet. Mrs. Grandberry was clearly shaken by the incident and began watching for shadows in staircases whenever we walked the streets. For days, I grappled with the physics of it all—how quickly the woman had spun, like a top whose cord had been ripped from behind. I'd have more than a few occasions to witness this spectacle in the coming years, as purse snatchings became as commonplace on the Hill as in the rest of Harlem.

While Pop grew more vigilant with each new sign of the neighborhood's decay, nothing deterred Daisy from her Saturday routine. Draped in black mink, rings turned palm-side so as not to draw too much attention, she'd walk to and from the train station on Saint Nicholas Avenue, nodding at the familiar faces of neighborhood kids, working folk, and welfare moms hanging out on the stoops, or to the men standing outside neighborhood dives like Lundy's, which stayed open all day and all night and attracted a broad swath of local characters, from the hardworking and hard drinking to the nefarious. Only once did I see her show concern. We were standing on the subway platform when a thuggish teenager started eyeing us. Daisy calmly reached into her big black leather pocketbook, pulled out a letter opener, flashed it menacingly, and then folded it defiantly under her crossed arms, pausing for a good long look in his direction. The train pulled in and we boarded without him.

Money was becoming tight. With two sons in private school and a third on the way to one, Pop was losing patience with Daisy's empty promises to rein in her spending. His state salary was modest and, by 1968, he had already sold the last of the Harlem properties that he'd inherited from our grandfather. Some, like the Jewish fraternity house Phi Epsilon Pi, had been sold for a fraction of their worth. There were no more rainy-day funds to dip into. For months, Pop had been threatening to cut off Daisy's credit line; this was the period when married women weren't issued charge cards in their own names or even given a bank loan without a husband cosigner (and blacks were often singled out as bad risks on the files of major downtown department stores). "Do what you want," he'd tell her, "but I'm not going to pay for it."

For a while, they played cat and mouse with the charge cards. He'd confiscate them. She'd ingratiate herself into getting them back—just this once, for this special occasion—but invariably returned with more than they had agreed on. She made sure to bring home at least one nice item for him, but he was tiring of her machinations. Finally, after one of her more memorable sprees, he cut up the E. J. Korvette and Gimbels cards. The damage was minimal. She simply spent more time, and money, at B. Altman, where her credit line was still good. In for a penny, in for a pound, was the way she saw it.

FIGURE 1 George Edmund Haynes in Washington, D.C., circa 1918.
Courtesy of Bruce D. Haynes.

FIGURE 2 George Edmund Haynes and his son George Jr., circa 1918.
Courtesy of Bruce D. Haynes.

FIGURE 3 Elizabeth Ross Haynes ("Rossi") in front of 411 Convent
Avenue, circa 1951. Courtesy of Bruce D. Haynes.

FIGURE 4 George Haynes Jr., late 1940s. Courtesy of Bruce D. Haynes.

FIGURE 5 George Haynes Jr. in front of 411 Convent Avenue. Courtesy of Bruce D. Haynes.

FIGURE 6 Daisy A. Haynes, circa 1948. This portrait always sat on George Jr.'s desk. Courtesy of Bruce D. Haynes.

FIGURE 7 Daisy A. Haynes with firstborn George Haynes III, circa 1952.
Courtesy of Bruce D. Haynes.

SEASON'S
GREETINGS

Haynes Jrs. Announce Birth
of Bruce Daniel.   11-20-60

FIGURE 8 Bruce Daniel Haynes's birth announcement, 1960.
Courtesy of Bruce D. Haynes.

FIGURE 9 Alan Ross Haynes in Boy Scouts uniform, circa 1963.
Courtesy of Bruce D. Haynes.

FIGURE 10 George Jr. and Daisy Haynes, Christmas 1970. Courtesy of
Bruce D. Haynes.

FIGURE 11 Bruce Daniel Haynes in summer 1970, age 9.
Courtesy of Bruce D. Haynes.

FIGURE 12 Alan Ross Haynes in his home in Yonkers, circa 1974.
Courtesy of Bruce D. Haynes.

FIGURE 13 Bruce Daniel Haynes in front of the portrait of George
Edmund Haynes in 2010.
Photo by Jim Wilson for the *New York Times*, © *New York Times*/Redux.

5

STEPPING OUT

MALCOLM X towered over me when I entered my brother
George's bedroom. The poster was mesmerizing. Malcolm, larger than life, was speaking from a podium,
biting down on his lower lip, his index finger lifted skyward toward
the caption: "We declare the right on this earth . . . to be a
human being, to be respected as a human being, to be given the
right of a human being in this society, on this earth, in this
day, which we intend to bring into existence BY ANY MEANS
NECESSARY."

This iconic image of black male defiance was in stark contrast
to the father who came to the breakfast table each morning. My
mother typically prepared oatmeal and half-slices of grapefruit,
and Pop often complained that she deliberately gave George the
bigger slice. She would scoff and tell him he was being ridiculous, but he'd measure it out with his hand. "Just look at it!" he
insisted. For Pop, the wedge signified all that Daisy was withholding from him. An Oedipal struggle played itself out in re-
verse, until George removed himself as a rival.

Everywhere George went that summer, he kept running into
a striking girl with almond eyes. He had noticed her in his poetry
class at City College and now found himself clerking beside

her at the Social Security Administration offices down on 125th Street. It was 1967 and George was seventeen—three years younger than his new interest, Sandra—yet with his full beard and broad build, he could easily pass for older. He worked hard to impress her, discussing Malcolm and Fanon and Coltrane.

After a few weeks, he mustered the nerve to ask her out, taking her to hear Miles Davis at Count Basie's Lounge, on 132nd Street and Seventh Avenue. Basie's was a small, intimate club, with just enough room to squeeze in a small stage at the back, a modest bar along one wall, and a few dozen small round tables that barely fit two drinks and an ashtray. Miles had become the epitome of cool and was all the rage in Harlem. He looked sharp that night, in a crisp dress shirt (open collar) and suit pants, but he had barely warmed up before he walked off in disgust (as was becoming his custom), leaving the rest of the quartet bewildered and the uptown crowd fuming. Still, the Bacardi and vibes kept flowing between George and Sandy, long after Miles's exit. Within weeks, they were talking about getting their own pad together.

I still don't understand my parents' laissez-faire attitude toward George's departure, given their high expectations for his future. They had always been so vigilant about his schoolwork. Now they put up little resistance when he proposed moving out, during his junior year of high school. Pop continued to pay the hefty tuition fees at Horace Mann, and even took out a $3,000 loan from Harlem's Freedom National Bank—the city's first black-owned bank—to help George set up an art studio on the first floor, which had long been vacated by Dolly.

Thus began yet another phase in our home's transformation. Mom seemed happy to support George's new business venture—named Studio Nefertiti—along with his move to the valley, so long as he remained in school. "They let me get away with hell," he told me years later. Perhaps, with George's mental illness surfacing, they felt that they had pushed too hard and were now overcompensating. Or perhaps they reassured themselves that he would come home soon, once he discovered how tough the real world was. Maybe his request didn't seem so unreasonable; after all, Pop, who had grown up in a dual-career household, had been a latchkey kid from the time he was in elementary school. Besides, my parents had no idea that George planned to move in with Sandy, and he went to great lengths to conceal it from them.

For the next three years, he clerked at Arthur Brown & Bro., the art supply store in midtown Manhattan, earning just enough to pay the rent. He worked out a special arrangement with the headmaster at Horace Mann to stretch his senior year over two school years, taking all his classes in the mornings and clerking in the afternoons. He had already decided he was going to be an artist and was producing most of the art for the student-run magazine at Horace Mann.

The experience at Arthur Brown's was invaluable. Sometimes George took me to 125th Street to sketch my portrait, hoping to drum up some business. His setup consisted of an easel, a box of pastels, a few charcoal pencils, two folding chairs, and a little sign advertising his services: four dollars for a profile; ten for a full portrait. I found those afternoons mortifying. I've always hated to be the center of attention, and here I was, on one of the busiest streets in the city, on display like a statue. Hundreds if not thousands of people passed by us every hour, and many stopped to look—first at me, and then my likeness—a little black boy in charcoal pencil with a near-perfect Afro.

When George wasn't studying, working, or sketching, he was reading about ancient Egypt. He had become interested in African art and history in his early teen years and had amassed an impressive collection of books on Egyptology, many of which he purchased from the National Memorial African Bookstore, the epicenter of black intellectual life in Harlem and the most influential black bookstore in the country. It was located on Seventh Avenue and 125th Street—later known as "the Corner" or "African Square" because of its long tradition of drawing soapbox orators, political agitators, and street preachers—and it served as a political hub for black radicals and organizers, including Malcolm X. The store was owned and operated by Lewis Michaux, a Harlem activist and bibliophile who had gained the respect of black progressives, such as W. E. B. Du Bois and George E. Haynes, and radicals alike. Known affectionately as "the Professor," Michaux attracted a loyal clientele, championed famous writers and artists, and hosted international leaders.

A native of Virginia, Michaux had arrived in New York City in the early 1920s with one book—*Up from Slavery* by Booker T. Washington. He combed the basement collections of Harlemites for books by or about blacks and peddled his wares from a pushcart for the next decade, until he saved enough to open a small store on 125th Street. The location proved auspicious, because this strip would become the commercial center of Harlem. By the mid-1960s, he had amassed some 150,000 books, strewn about on tables and stacked floor to ceiling along the walls.

Michaux had known our grandfather, who frequently shopped at his store, and spoke of him with great reverence. He introduced George to some of the great saviors of black history, like J. A. Rogers, but also to edgier writers like Frantz Fanon, the psychiatrist and anticolonialist who wrote, in *The Wretched of the Earth*, that violence was a necessary means of liberation from colonization. Fanon was becoming the rage among self-styled revolutionaries and assorted Marxists, Maoists, Soledad Brothers, Black Panthers, and the occasional Castro sympathizer, who were likely to patronize the more radical Liberation Bookstore, another Harlem landmark, located ten blocks north.

George came to idolize this African-centric man with the baby Afro, balding at the top, and the star-and-crescent pillbox hat. He began spending Saturdays at the shop. Whenever there was a lull, Michaux would lead George on a winding trail through the piled books to a little room in the back, where Malcolm X had once been a regular and Michaux now kept his Black Hall of Fame— portraits of black American heroes, African heads of state, and, oddly, Dwight D. Eisenhower and Franklin D. Roosevelt.

In 1967, the National Memorial African Bookstore was torn down to make way for the Harlem State Office Building—a major event signaling the advent of urban revitalization in Harlem. By then, George was becoming swept up in the burgeoning Black Arts Movement, which merged black art with Black Power. The movement is considered to have formally launched in March 1965, one month after the assassination of Malcolm X, when poet, playwright, and music critic LeRoi Jones (soon to be Amiri Baraka) moved from Greenwich Village to Harlem to establish the Black Arts Repertory Theater/School. Jones had recently written the racially charged play *Dutchman*, which presaged a militant artistic vision that would characterize the Black Arts Movement. "We want poems that kill" was its manifesto.

Although the Black Arts Movement was pronounced the "aesthetic and spiritual sister of the Black Power concept," George still had one political foot in the civil rights agenda of Martin Luther King Jr. During his senior year of high school, he became involved in the Poor People's Campaign of 1968, which was organized by King's Southern Christian Leadership Conference. Unlike earlier civil rights initiatives, which focused on desegregation and racial equality, this campaign would advocate for the needs of all poor people, regardless of race. It proposed a radical platform for an "economic bill of rights," under which the federal government would award $30 billion to fight poverty and would commit to providing full employment for all Americans. The campaign was to culminate in a second March on Washington, on April 22, 1968. To further pressure President Lyndon B. Johnson and Congress to pass legislation, conference leaders planned to build a giant tent city, called Resurrection City, on the Washington Mall, where demonstrators were to remain until their demands were met. Just weeks before the march was to take place, King was shot and killed in Memphis while defending the rights of striking sanitation workers. Campaigners decided to move forward with the march (postponing it by a month), but George would not be among them. Two boxes of Poor People's Campaign buttons collected dust in George's room.

During this period, George drew a self-portrait that foreshadowed his journey into Islam but also reflected his wrestling with the role of violence in the quest for liberation. In the upper right corner floats Malcolm's head, his eyes cast downward; at the bottom left is a muscular line drawing of Martin staring off into the distance. George, august and celestial, commands the center, his disembodied head suspended in a halo. A trinity of revolutionaries hovers just outside the circle. The first is dressed in a robe and head covering and strikes a peaceful, contemplative look while he loads a rifle; he bears an uncanny resemblance to George. The second, a hip-looking brother with dark shades, holds a rifle across his body and stands in an "at ease" military pose. The last is a woman with an Angela Davis Afro; an M16 is draped across her body and a broad, warm smile beams out into the future. Years later, George explained that the peaceful man wielding the gun represented Jesus. "The way I saw it then was that if Jesus came back today he would be a revolutionary. He's contemplating whether to use his gun, while the others have already decided what to do."

George had developed the strongest race consciousness in the family and saw it as his job to school me in the new black-centric perspective that was growing across the nation. He bought me a children's book on black cowboys long before I learned to read. On our Sunday trips to Grandma Mattie in New Jersey, he'd point out the Sambo's restaurant on Route 42 and warn me to never eat there. He explained to me what each color—black, red, and green—represented in the black liberation flag, which was boldly displayed in the windows of stores up and down 125th Street. Although the flag was a sign of the new black attitude, there was nothing new about the flag. The Universal Negro Improvement Association and African Communities League had adopted it in 1920 in response to the popular white ditty "Every Race Has a Flag but the Coon."

George wanted to be sure I knew that we were now Black and no longer Negro, but at eight years old, I was much more concerned about fitting in at my new white school than raising my black consciousness. I was already self-conscious about the raised, bumpy skin on my thumb. I hid it as much as I could, but there were times when it had to come out. Someone would invariably ask, "What's wrong with your thumb?" I made excuses, laughed it off, but I was certain that everyone had guessed the truth: at eight years old, I still sucked my thumb.

Many of my new downtown classmates were nouveau riche and lived in swank Manhattan neighborhoods—Sutton Place, Yorkville, and the Upper West Side. A few, like me, were middle class. Still fewer were black. For nearly all of them, 110th Street marked the boundary between light and darkness, rich and poor. For this short, slightly built kid, coming from Harlem gave me just the edge I needed to invoke fear in playground skirmishes. Some kids, as well as their parents, were taken aback when they learned that my family owned a brownstone in Harlem. "A brownstone in Harlem?" they'd ask, or "You mean to say that your parents are married?" This question always struck me as strange because most of my parent's friends were married and lived in homes at least as nice as our own. The stereotypes seemed to run in only one direction; when I ran across my old classmates from Harlem, I was never accused of "acting white" for attending prep school. (Years later, however, I did get ribbed by my peers for listening to the Grateful Dead and the Rolling Stones. Now *that* was acting white!)

The transition from public to private school was humbling. Overnight, I had fallen from the top of my class at P.S. 186 to the bottom ranks at Emerson. My math skills were rudimentary and, although I had always thought of myself as an advanced reader, I was only average in my new school. Still, the teachers were outstanding, classes were small—fifteen students on average, less than half the size of my first- and second-grade classes at P.S. 186—and I caught up quickly.

By fourth grade, I was taking public transportation to school. In my navy blue knit pants, crisp jacket, and tie, and with a green canvas knapsack stuffed with books, I boarded the Convent Avenue bus that stopped just across the street from our home. I remember staring into the sleepy faces of old black men and women who rode in the early morning. They seemed to recognize that I was headed into a world they had only come to know from behind a mop. As the bus crossed 110th Street, they exited in twos and threes, while white folks boarded for destinations farther downtown. I got off at 65th Street and caught the crosstown bus heading east.

Despite the cultural capital that I brought to Emerson—my parents took me to the same museums and plays that my classmates went to, and they bought me all the junior classics to read—there were nagging reminders that I was different. One cold November morning, as I waited outside our house for the bus, I watched our neighbor Ms. Gallo, a heavyset, middle-aged black woman, come out from her basement apartment in her bathrobe. In an almost gingerly way, she stepped onto the sidewalk, dropped her robe, and strutted buck naked up the block. My parents, who were watching from upstairs, rushed me into the vestibule until the bus arrived.

Within a few years, I was developing the speech patterns that one of my old friends from the projects referred to as "that 'bougie' accent," which reflected the unique cultural milieu of middle-class black New York. Class consciousness among black Harlemites was very much alive when I was growing up. In *Harlemworld: Doing Race and Class in Contemporary Black America*, the urban anthropologist John Jackson talks about how class is signified in the streets of Harlem by the different voices and styles employed. Class is about more than where you're located; it's something that is performed. How you walk and how you talk signifies your class.

I learned to perform the middle class at home—speak Standard English, cover your mouth when you yawn, say "excuse me" for any bodily sounds. I was being groomed for survival downtown, in a white and privileged world. But those very behaviors put me at a clear disadvantage uptown. Luckily, my brothers kept me moored to the cultural lingo of Harlem. I learned to code-switch, blend in and out, on a dime.

Over time, most black inflections faded from my diction. "Where are you from?" both blacks and whites would ask. "From Harlem," I'd tell them. "No, where is your family from?" "We're from Harlem." "No, no, where're you *from*?" I later realized they meant "What island are you from?" They had assumed I was West Indian, the "model" minority of black America. The idea of "West Indian exceptionalism" was advanced by the black economist Thomas Sowell, who attributed the higher incomes of West Indians, along with their overrepresentation in professional occupations, to their values and behavior patterns, thus undermining "the proposition that color is a fatal handicap in the American economy." The values of black Americans held them back, he argued, whereas those of West Indians catapulted them forward. Sadly, even black Americans sometimes internalized these cultural stereotypes about success, and thus many took my Standard English and bourgeois accent as a proxy for my foreignness.

In truth, I often felt like a marginal man. Having been born at the tail end of the baby boom, on a block that people had moved to postwar, most of the kids in the neighborhood were from Alan and George's generation. By the time I came around, everyone on the block was getting old, and because the neighborhood was turning dangerous during this same time, I wasn't allowed to go outside and play with kids my age. By seven, I was attending school outside of Harlem and had few interactions with my old classmates. My brothers had been entrenched in Harlem institutions like the YMCA, the Boy Scouts, and the church (by the time I was born, my parents had stopped going to church) and had developed lasting friendships from those experiences. They were vested in Harlem in a way that I could never be. Both uptown and downtown, I was on the outside looking in. Eventually, sociology provided me with a language to talk about the things I was destined to only observe.

Though I was one of only a handful of black students at Emerson, the kids were very accepting and I made friends quickly. For the first time, I had playdates and sleepovers and went to birthday parties. I was invited to country homes in the Catskills and Connecticut. I learned to play spin the bottle and, later, a variation called seven minutes in heaven—where a boy and girl are locked together in a closet for seven minutes. The point of the game was to give boys and girls who had crushes on one another a chance to get together without having to admit that they had a crush. Of course, selection was one-sided, and we often ended up with someone we didn't want to be alone with.

I wasn't able to reciprocate the generosity of my classmates. My world was harder to explain. The house, like my parents, was showing signs of emotional stress. The paint was starting to peel in the hallway, and the house was dark and dungeon-like. After

Mrs. Grandberry left, the blinds and the heavy gold drapes remained closed all day—to preserve heat and prevent would-be burglars from peering in. Most difficult to explain to an outsider was the back room, where I slept. My new friends had their own bedrooms, which were filled with toys and books and where other children played when they came to visit. Where would my friends play? In the back room, with its card table for eating meals and the tiny black-and-white television set, which rested on a larger, broken black-and-white television set? My friends had big color televisions and entire rooms for dining. And I couldn't take them to my brothers' old rooms on the third floor, which were now coated with dust, flakes of lead-based paint dangling from the ceiling. Only my closest friends from downtown, whom I trusted to never judge or betray me, were invited into my home.

Despite the mounting chaos at home, I remember the years at Emerson as among the happiest of my life. I learned to imagine melting like ice, make a rattlesnake from papier-mâché, play the recorder, and even dance the waltz. We had famous people, like James Earl Jones, visit our classrooms, and many of my classmates had famous parents, such as the actor Robert Morse. Some classmates, like Jeffrey Toobin, went on to become famous themselves.

In many ways, we were being groomed for a world of money and status. We had French conversation each day with Madame Angiel and took yearly trips to her French camp in Woodstock. One year we were taken to a fancy French restaurant for a five-course meal. We were expected to order in French and to display proper etiquette, such as knowing which fork and spoon to use for each course. There was a presumption that we were already exposed to such bourgeois conventions at home and that the school was merely building upon them. Here, too, I was not ill-prepared. Whenever we visited Grandma Mattie in New Jersey, she prepared an appetizer (always a fruit cocktail crowned with a maraschino cherry), a main course, and a dessert. A separate fork was assigned to each, and the plates were cleared after each course.

Unlike most of New York's private schools, where integration was achieved by handing out scholarships to poor kids from the ghetto, Emerson drew black kids from the middle class. And the administration and teaching staff were unusually diverse for a school that served the upper echelons of Manhattan. The principal of Emerson, Mrs. Gadsden, was black, as was my fourth-grade teacher, Mrs. Caution (the name says it all!), and our gym teacher—a professional dancer who had his own troupe uptown, the Tommy Hawkins Dancers. Mr. Hawkins knew next to nothing about basketball, which he coached, and his dribbling skills were embarrassing, but he could leap four feet in the air, effortlessly, to dunk the ball, and he earned the respect of all the boys, despite his effeminate mannerisms. Over the years, Mr. Hawkins became a role model for me. He was short and dark-skinned like me but he had the presence of someone far larger. He was strong, angular, and buffed. He had charisma and a commanding voice, and he walked with a graceful confidence that bespoke years of self-conscious, purposeful movement.

The new activist spirit of the 1960s brought sweeping changes to old civil rights organizations. The National Urban League—created by my grandfather to help southern black migrants transition to the industrial North—began its own transition, in the early 1960s, under the direction of Whitney M. Young Jr. To a new generation of leaders, the social reform models of the past looked obsolete in the face of postwar urban ghettoization. Equal access alone would never eradicate the chasms fashioned over decades and brought to national attention by Lyndon B. Johnson's Kerner Commission: male underemployment; inadequate, overcrowded, and segregated housing; declining and dilapidated public schools; under-resourced libraries and youth clubs; and lack of access to health care and childcare—not to mention the fear of police brutality, which told you to stay in your place, on your side of town. What folks needed now was an aggressive reform agenda, and Young proposed a domestic "Marshall Plan" to tackle inner-city poverty, calling for $145 billion in federal aid to cities over ten years. President Johnson incorporated much of Young's model into his War on Poverty initiative. Young was also successful in persuading corporate America and major foundations to support self-help programs for education, jobs, housing, and family rehabilitation. This became the cornerstone of the newly refashioned organization.

By 1965, the National Urban League had grown in size, from 300 to more than 1,200 employees, and its budget had increased tenfold. Young also oversaw the league's shift in business ties, from the industrial to the corporate sector, cultivating relationships with business leaders and CEOs and pushing them to hire more blacks. He grappled with striking a fine balance between marshaling financial support from whites and selling out to them, just as my grandfather, George Haynes, had done half a century before. Although Young had been a major organizer of the 1963 March on Washington, he—along with NAACP executive secretary Roy Wilkins—worked closely with President John F. Kennedy to tone down any fiery rhetoric (anticipated by the Student Nonviolent Coordinating Committee and the Congress of Racial Equality, or CORE) and to limit the focus of the march to rallying support for the civil rights bill before Congress. It is reported that Student Nonviolent Coordinating Committee chairman John Lewis was forced to rewrite his original speech.

Like my grandfather, Young often came under fire from more aggressive community leaders for his ties to the white power structure. And while he reproached them for their more radical tactics, he also warned white business and civic leaders that only substantive gains for blacks would curtail civil unrest and violence. Significant inroads were made under Young's leadership. Federal and private grants funded an ambitious agenda that included job training, open housing, minority executive recruitment, and "street academies"—the earliest alternative schools for high school dropouts. As black communities across the nation struggled for their survival, the league responded to a growing urban crisis by shifting its resources to direct services. And although the league had originally been funded through private dollars, government support now accounted for more than two-thirds of its budget.

Along with the cries for equal rights came racial unrest, and New York exploded long before the riots of 1967 swept the country. In July 1964, thousands of Harlem residents took to the streets after James Powell, a fifteen-year-old black boy, was shot and killed by a white off-duty police officer. The protest, initially organized by CORE, had begun peacefully, as blacks demonstrated outside Harlem's 28th Precinct—on Eighth Avenue, near 122nd Street—but erupted as protesters clashed with the police. The violence soon spread to the largely black Brooklyn neighborhood of Bedford-Stuyvesant. After nearly a week of looting, arson, and run-ins with local police, one person was dead and hundreds were injured. The 1964 riots came on the heels of more than four years of nonviolent efforts across the country to effect change in government policies, beginning with the lunch counter sit-ins in Greensboro, North Carolina. The perceived failure of these tactics helped to create the conditions for more violent strategies.

By the late 1960s, Pop was frequently lecturing George and Alan on how to protect themselves from police brutality. A law enforcement officer himself, he was well acquainted with the routine transgressions of his fellow "peace officers," especially when it came to confronting black males. "Yes, Officer; no, Officer" was the only acceptable response when being stopped by the police. "Make no sudden moves," he cautioned them. "Keep your hands where they can be seen, and don't reach for your wallet until you're instructed—and when you do reach for it, move slowly and deliberately."

Not that Alan could be a menace to anyone. At sixteen, he was becoming an "Afro-hippie" who looked like he would have been more at home in Berkeley than in Harlem. He played the guitar and bass and was into rock-and-roll jam bands, smoking pot, building guitars, riding bikes, and saving stray animals. Yet, at six foot two, with his large Afro and dark aviator shades, he was a visible target for cops who were none too skilled at distinguishing between a black militant and a black flower child.

Being the closest in age, Alan always got stuck babysitting me. It couldn't have been his idea of a good time, but there was no one I would have rather been with. We'd curl up together on the floor in front of the television, he stretching out on his side and making a perfect giant pillow for me. Life didn't get any better than that. I idolized Alan and was so proud that this tall, cool guy was my big brother. Seven years, four months, and eight days older than me, I rattled off annoyingly. It still trips off my tongue today.

He always seemed to pick the perfect TV show or the best food to eat—candy buttons, vanilla fudge ice cream, and brown edge cookies. If he ate it, I ate it. If he said it, I said it. I insisted that my mother buy me the Adidas sneakers with the stripes on the side, just like he wore. I didn't just want to be *like* Alan; I wanted to *be* Alan. Sometimes he let me hang out when his friends came over. We'd race slot cars and have water fights. He let me crawl into bed with him when I had nightmares. Every once in a while, he tired of the burden of watching over me and would disappear with his friends up to his playroom. Those moments of abandonment were devastating. I remember crying outside his room, at the top of the stairs. After a few moments, he'd come out and sit next to me. "Nobody loves me anymore!" I sniffled. "Come on, Brucie, you know that's not true!" A little rub on my shoulder, a pat on the head, and everything would be all right again.

Alan was the emotive one in the family and the most comfortable with physical closeness, which made me all the more dependent on his hugs and his cuddles. My mom was the type who would kiss the air as she leaned away from you, and she responded to declarations of love with her signature line: "Thank you, dahlin'." Pop, meanwhile, had been raised in a Victorian-starch household, where liberal displays of affection were seen as somewhat crass. My parents showed their love by what they did for us, and they did plenty. Still, Alan's kind of love was what I needed.

Even as I grew too big to cry, Alan never grew immune to my entreaties. He and his friends might lock me out of some secret meeting but, sooner or later, my cries of abandonment would break his resistance down. On one occasion, I was invited in to taste an amazing strawberry-flavored concoction. It was years before I figured out that it had been Strawberry Nestlé's Quik.

When I was eight, Alan bought me my first rock albums— Steppenwolf's *The Second* and Jimi Hendrix's *Axis: Bold as Love*. I played them endlessly on my little silver record player and wowed my new playmates downtown when I brought them to school. One of my peak memories as a kid was riding on Alan's shoulders. I had always been a little kid, the first in line at school (when teachers still made kids line up by height), but atop my six-foot-two brother I towered over the world! Tall enough to whack my head on the station signs in the subway. Once, as we

were waiting on the subway platform—me, giddy at nine feet
in the air—Alan brought us right to the precipice and daringly
began teetering along the little yellow border. I panicked and
covered his eyes with my hands, thinking somehow I could prevent us from falling if he couldn't see. He lurched for a second
before he managed to pull my hands away. That was one of the
only times I remember him getting cross with me.

Alan began spending less time at home. Like most youth of
the sixties, he was becoming politicized into the struggle for
equal rights. He was now attending the progressive and largely
white Walden School, where Andrew Goodman—one of three
Freedom Riders slain in Mississippi in the summer of 1964—
had been a student a few years before. Alan began talking about
going down South himself and joining the voter registration
drive, a prospect more terrifying to my parents than if he had
joined the Black Panthers. At fifteen, he joined the Congress of
Racial Equality, in part because his friend's father, Floyd Mc-
Kissick, had just replaced James Farmer as its national director.
Pop—an ardent supporter of the old civil rights agenda—didn't
trust McKissick or his politics, and he complained whenever
Alan went over to their house.

Pop's instincts turned out to be dead-on. McKissick would
transform CORE from an interracial civil rights organization
committed to integration and nonviolence to a staunch advocate
of the Black Power movement, purging the word *multiracial* from
its charter and whites from its organization. McKissick left
CORE in 1968 and passed the torch to his close ally Roy Innis.
The organization continued its radical-conservative turn, pro-
claiming itself a black nationalist organization while supporting
Richard Nixon in his bid for the presidency. Innis was drawn
to the GOP because of its support for community policing and
community control. But he struck a devil's bargain: in exchange
for self-determination, his support gave the Republicans license

to enact policies that ensured the continued segregation and impoverishment of black communities.

After McKissick left CORE, he launched Soul City, an integrated community planned for a strip of farmland in Warren County, North Carolina. Framed as the brainchild of the kinder, gentler party under Richard Nixon, it was really a GOP scheme to secure black votes while returning blacks to unwanted rural areas. McKissick's son, Alan's friend Floyd Jr., would go on to become a state senator in North Carolina. My parents had similar aspirations for Alan and sent him to Washington, DC, during the summer of 1968, to intern as a Senate page. He returned uninspired, still clinging to his dream of becoming a musician.

Alan was immersed in the multiracial world of rock and roll but, like many black youths of the sixties, he practiced sympathetic militancy. In April 1969, when a group of black, Puerto Rican, and white students took over the South Campus and Klapper Hall of the City College of New York (CCNY), demanding more diversity among the faculty and in the curriculum, Alan brandished an aluminum billy club in a defiant show of "us against them" solidarity mixed with real fear of police retaliation.

George was at the helm of these protests and one of the key organizers of the High School Coalition—a group that ignited student protests throughout the city and advocated the takeover of high schools and colleges. The coalition was a decentralized network of cells in which no one group or individual claimed responsibility. "There was no leadership you could point your finger at. That was part of the strategy," he recalled. George remained active during the two-week takeover of CCNY, at one point running the college radio station and commandeering the Gestetner (an old-style mimeograph machine) at Klapper Hall to deliver news to the student masses.

Our parents had no inkling of George's involvement. Nor did they know that he had brought me to CCNY—just ten blocks south of our home—at the height of the protests, leading me through the campus and into the student dorms and administration buildings that were now under siege. Everybody seemed to know my big brother, and I felt so proud to be trailing behind him. The campus was electric—students in dashikis and Afros, African drum circles, assorted smoke wafting through the air. By the time the students agreed to vacate, two weeks later, the administration had agreed to a controversial open enrollment plan, and the university's president, Dr. Buell Gallagher, had resigned. Thanks to data from the U.S. Department of Labor and the award-winning research of sociologists Paul Attewell and David Lavin, we now know that the university's new policy was successful. Some 70 percent of all disadvantaged women admitted to CUNY in the early 1970s graduated and boosted their incomes while improving the educational success of their children.

High school and college students weren't the only ones "down with the cause." Radical was the new chic in the late sixties, and white socialites and intellectuals began courting black and brown liberation groups like the Black Panthers, the Young Lords, and, in California, the striking grape workers. In his wicked satire for *New York* magazine, Tom Wolfe chronicled a dinner party thrown at Leonard Bernstein's Park Avenue duplex for the Black Panther Party. Wolfe muses on the challenges of finding white servants (it would be unthinkable to have blacks serving at these events) and whether the Panthers "like little Roquefort cheese morsels wrapped in crushed nuts this way, and asparagus tips in mayonnaise dabs, and *meatballs petites au Coq Hardi*, all of which are at this very moment being offered to them on gadrooned silver platters by maids in black uniforms with hand-ironed white aprons."

6

DO FOR YOURSELF

GEORGE started bringing tiny bean pies to the house, along with copies of *Muhammad Speaks* that he'd purchased from the smartly dressed bowtie brothers on 125th Street. Although the newspaper was the financial backbone of the Nation of Islam (NOI), it appealed to a much broader segment of black New Yorkers with its exposés of police brutality and reports on urban uprisings. George was drawn to the paper for its articles on how to get and keep a job and how to stand proud and independent as a black man, a battle he continued to wage with our father and, later, with his wife, Sandy.

Although both of my parents were staunch integrationists, Mom registered little disapproval of her son's new interest; she admired Malcolm X and had even attended his funeral, in Harlem, in 1965. Pop, however, denounced the Nation and ridiculed their claims of "white devils" being invented in a laboratory by an evil genius named Dr. Yakub. Yet beneath the rhetoric of the white devil lay a very conservative agenda. Economic self-sufficiency without government help was widely advocated by the NOI and the GOP alike. The "do for yourself, pick yourself up by your bootstraps" ethos that promised to strengthen black communities without the paternalism of whites resonated with many young men like George. Unfortunately, the Nation's rhetoric was not matched by practical business strategies.

Three years would pass before George made the leap from rhetoric to practice. By then, he had graduated from Horace Mann, married Sandy, and spent a year at Bensalem, a new experimental college at Fordham University, with no set curriculum, requirements, or grades, where students and faculty shared power in running the school. The school received attention from *Esquire*, the *Saturday Review*, and *Look*, which described it as "the farthest out college in the U.S. today." Bensalem was a school without walls, and students could attend classes anywhere they wished—or opt to take no classes at all—defining for themselves what an education meant. Some students and faculty formed communes together. Others traveled or launched their own artistic ventures. George studied the visual arts at New York University, learning everything from silk screening to running a printing press.

In 1969, all three of us were attending private, progressive schools. My parents had long been advocates of progressive education, with its historical commitments to racial and economic diversity. Pop himself had attended high school at the Ethical Culture School, in New York, which the U.S. Bureau of the Census ranked, in 1916, as "one of the foremost experimental stations in educational matters" and which had long extolled the virtues of an education for all children, regardless of their background, race, or class. Alan and George had both attended the experimental Public School 129, where students were observed from behind one-way mirrors by researchers from the City College of New York School of Education. The school was piloting the Science Research Associates reading program, which allowed students to direct their own learning through a system of color-coded texts. The pilot was so successful that the program was adopted for the entire New York City public school system. (George's reading skills soared under the program, and by the time he entered P.S. 143, in eighth grade, he was reading at a twelfth-grade level.)

Alan was sixteen now and thriving at the Walden School, which had a first-rate performing arts program. The school was widely known for its antiauthoritarian approach to learning. Students received no grades and called teachers by their first names. Competition was minimized while creativity was nurtured. Alan studied both the guitar and bass and played in several rock-and-roll bands around the city.

Meanwhile, I was in my second year at Emerson and about to begin my own stint as a musician. My mother had always believed that I was destined for stardom, but she didn't know where the opportunity would come from. When a jazz pianist friend told her about the Little Church Around the Corner, she arranged for an audition. The choirmaster played a series of notes on the piano and asked me to sing them back. That was the beginning of my singing career; for the next four years I spent every Tuesday and Thursday evening and all of my Sundays singing in the church choir. We sang Gregorian chants, Bach cantatas, and Handel's *Messiah*. I sang with the Berkshire Boy Choir and with New York Pro Musica, an ensemble that specialized in medieval and Renaissance music and was known for its revival of the *Play of Daniel* and the *Play of Herod*, which we performed each year at the Cloisters museum.

Throughout my years at the Little Church Around the Corner, I performed in all of the big Episcopal churches of New York City and in most of the major concert venues, including Carnegie Hall, Philharmonic Hall (later called Avery Fisher Hall), and Alice Tully Hall, often under the conductor Pierre Boulez. One summer I traveled to Romania; another summer I toured the country with Leonard Bernstein.

One of the perks of being a choirboy was the weekly stipend, which increased every year. By the time I was twelve, I was earning $120 a month. Pretty good spending change for a kid! The other benefit was the recreational facilities. The church had a pool table, ping-pong table, and small basketball court. For four and a half years, two days a week, I was the first to get to church and the last to leave. By the time my stint ended, I was a pretty mean opponent in all three games.

Our choirmaster, Stuart Gardner, was a prominent figure in the sacred music world of the Episcopal Church. He had an extraordinary zest for life and opened my eyes to how people could live their lives. He had a beach house in Connecticut, right on Long Island Sound, and would invite his favorites to go out there for weekends. I remember whizzing down the Henry Hudson Parkway with him at seventy miles per hour, the sunroof open, classical music blaring, his arms outstretched as he conducted the orchestra, all while navigating the curves of the tree-lined roads. At night, he barbecued burgers and steaks and let us drink burgundy. He immersed us in a world of European high culture and gave us the freedom to be adults.

By my fourth year in the choir, I had become a fairly strong singer and was made backup soloist. There were two occasions that year when I sang solo, and neither was a great success. One was in Romania. We'd been touring for about two weeks when many of the kids, including the lead soloist, began complaining of nausea and light-headedness, which we later learned were symptoms of calcium deficiency. I, who was gorging on the rich Romanian chocolate, stayed healthy. What did me in that evening was the white chino pants we'd been given for the performance. They were a little big, and I could feel them sagging throughout the solo. I became preoccupied with them, imagining that everyone was focused on my sagging pants. But, of course, it wasn't until the end of the solo, when I discreetly pulled them up, that everyone started to laugh. I was humiliated. The second solo was worse. I froze. I didn't have the emotional stamina to pull it off alone. I could belt it out when I was protected by the group, and

I could even sing duets but, despite what my mother saw in me, I wasn't meant for the limelight.

▼

George would never complete his degree at Bensalem. Like many of its students, he discovered the limits of self-regulation and became disillusioned with the lack of structure and direction. "It was a hippy-dippy place, something between a commune and a college. It was filled with artists and idealists but no real educators or professionals." Another factor was money. "They said you could take classes anywhere you wanted but never explained that it would cost extra." The classes at New York University hadn't been included in the tuition.

Although many students thrived in that environment—going on to respected graduate schools, and some winning enviable fellowships—nearly half of the student body left before graduating, and most of the faculty fled within one or two years. George left in 1970, after just one year.

Soon, he and Sandy were expecting their first child. Money was tight, and he wouldn't gain his inheritance from our grandfather for another few months, when he turned twenty-one. One day he was sitting in Wells Chicken and Waffles restaurant in Harlem's valley when he struck up a conversation with a man from Chicago. They discussed the Black Arts Movement, which was thriving in Chicago, as well as new opportunities for black artists. His new acquaintance mentioned in passing that George should look him up if he ever went out that way. Within weeks, George boarded a bus to Chicago, carrying little more than his art portfolio. His intent was to assess the art scene and send for Sandy and the baby once he secured a job.

He never did connect with the man from Chicago or make any art connections. Over the next six months, he mingled, partied, and shacked up with an eclectic assortment of folks, from spiritualists who astral traveled to Mars to jazz musicians who partied with the likes of Herbie Hancock. George subsisted by working the phone banks at the National Opinion Research Center, headquartered at the University of Chicago campus, but he spent more time conducting research on ancient Egypt than on American attitudes and preferences. Within four months, he was fired.

He returned to New York and to Sandy and took a job with Davis & Warshow, a plumbing supply company on Ludlow Street, in lower Manhattan. One day, about a year later, when his boss took him out for lunch, George was sure he was getting a promotion and a raise. He was half right. The company planned to promote him to manager of the fittings department. But it had no intention of raising his salary from a trainee's wages. George protested, respectfully at first, and the conversation turned testy. Even after he agreed to their terms, the relationship had soured. A few weeks later, he called in to request the next Saturday off and was told that if he took the day, it would be his last. He took the day.

Many young black men like George found themselves caught in dead-end jobs in the post–Civil Rights era. True, new federal legislation had brought massive institutional shifts and new opportunities for blacks, and George's generation was at the front line of this transition. A decade earlier, he never would have landed a supervisor position; most black men were confined to menial occupations, working as janitors, porters, dishwashers, elevator operators, and messengers. Now, any company with at least fifty workers was subject to regulation and could be sued for discrimination. Many employers actively sought black workers, some with a genuine commitment to integrating their workplaces. Yet some companies made perfunctory hires, looking only to shield themselves from government intervention. What better foil than a young, bright, middle-class black kid with a prep school background? The cream of the crop for a flunky's wages. And it was the best job George could get.

Over the next year, George bounced between jobs, supplementing his income with odd print jobs he ran from his Studio Nefertiti back home. By the time he met Brother William, he was working at Brownell Electro, an industrial wire company in the old Nabisco building on Tenth Avenue.

He had seen Brother William before—a tall, sharp-dressed brother in his midsixties—usually inside the small dry cleaning and tailor business on Convent Avenue, sitting at the window, making small talk with the manager, watching the days pass by. One day their gazes locked and Brother William motioned for George to come inside. He asked George if he had ever read *Muhammad Speaks*, pulling out a copy that he just happened to have handy. By now, George was well acquainted with the paper, and they talked about "Brother Malcolm (peace be upon him)" and Islam—the true religion of the black man in America. Brother William seemed to be an authority on black history, tossing out facts and figures that George had never come across, even at Michaux's bookstore. Fascinated with Brother William's steadfast certainty, George agreed to visit his mosque in the Bronx.

He was not prepared for the level of protocol and formality he found there. To his surprise, the mosque had the same rules as upscale midtown establishments: if a guest did not have a jacket, he was provided with one. This bourgeois kid from Convent Avenue felt embarrassed that he had to borrow one of the Nation's "guest jackets," an oversize garment that hung off him and made him feel like a charity case. He made sure he came prepared next time.

There were many next times. In 1972, George Edmund Haynes III became George 78X. The process for obtaining membership and a new name consisted of writing a "Savior's Letter" to the Chicago NOI headquarters. The letter, handwritten on unlined bond paper, was addressed to Elijah Muhammad and followed a set format:

> Dear Savior Allah, Our Deliverer: I have been attending the teachings of Islam by one of your Ministers, two or three times. I believe in It, and I bear witness that there is no God but Allah, and that Muhammad is Thy Servant and Apostle. I desire to reclaim my Own. Please give me my Original Name. My slave name is as follows: Name, Address

Any letters that were illegible or that had spelling, punctuation, or grammatical errors were rejected. Even the spacing on the page had to be perfect. For many young brothers, this was the first time that they had ever written a letter, and many had to rewrite theirs several times before they were accepted. Some were illiterate and had to trace each word from the template. The act itself was the initiation—a first step toward discipline and perfection. When the letter was accepted, the applicant was told to report to his local mosque to receive his X, which represented both an unknown quantity (the unknown African surname) and the unyoking of the past (ex-slave, ex–drug addict, ex-alcoholic).

George 78X was now expected to attend mosque three times a week—Wednesdays, Fridays, and Sundays—and to train with the Fruit of Islam each Saturday morning. Unlike most religious conversions, which required one to relinquish old practices before being welcomed into the fold, the doctrines of the Nation—the Supreme Wisdom Lessons—were introduced after one's acceptance into it. These lessons, also known as the "Lost-Found Lessons," were a set of Socratic-style dialogues between Master Fard Muhammad, the Nation's founder, and Elijah Muhammad, its messenger. Each lesson had to be committed to memory and recited verbatim before one could move on to the next. Also to be mastered were the *Actual Facts* about planet Earth—its diameter and circumference, its oceans, lakes, and rivers, its hills and mountains, islands and deserts, the speed of sound and light. For some, these lessons were the first introduction to modern geography and science. For George, whose mental illness was slowly taking hold, the rigid structure and discipline were comforting.

The highest level of teachings was contained in the mathematical theology of *The Problem Book*. Wrapped in each problem was a metaphor, the meaning of which was revealed in stages and only to the most advanced students. Some problems could take years to unwrap. Others would be revealed in a Fruit of Islam class or in a lecture with Minister Louis Farrakhan. "You memorized the question," George said, "and hopefully, sometime in your career as an FOI, the captain would teach you what it meant."

Like all neophytes, George 78X read Elijah Muhammad's *Message to the Blackman in America* and *How to Eat to Live*, which advocated eating one meal per day and eschewed pork, corn bread, sweet potatoes (which produced gas), and most other foods associated with the "slave diet." These prohibitions were part of a larger strategy to decolonize the Negro mind, severing the ties to his southern Christian roots.

George cut his Afro and food intake, donned the NOI uniform of dark suit and bow tie, and faithfully peddled *Muhammad Speaks*, although he rarely met his weekly quota of two hundred newspapers. With his impeccable education and writing skills, he quickly rose among the rank and file and was appointed secretary of his mosque. The Nation had a rigid, almost militaristic, hierarchy. Each mosque had a minister, captain, secretary, and investigator, each of whom reported to their counterpart at the next-highest echelon, which in New York was the borough. The structure was replicated at the city and national levels. George reported to the secretary for all of the Bronx, who in turn reported to the New York City secretary. The supreme minister was the Honorable Elijah Muhammad, the Messenger of Allah, who ran the NOI with absolute authority and appointed the minister and captain of each mosque.

As secretary of his mosque, George was responsible for reporting the "actual facts" to the minister. In this context, the actual facts referred to records of attendance—the number of members and visitors (called Lost-Founds) who had attended services that week, as well as the number of new recruits—and charity, the total financial contributions for the week.

All NOI officials—captains, lieutenants, and secretaries alike— were known as laborers and, as secretary of his mosque, George was required to attend weekly laborers' meetings with Minister Farrakhan. Although the assassination of el-Hajj Malik el-Shabazz, aka Malcolm X, had cast a cloud of suspicion over Farrakhan, he was never officially connected to the murder and was now recognized as the official spokesman for the Honorable Elijah Mohammad. George described Farrakhan as humble and soft-spoken, a far cry from the flamboyant orator who demonized the white man and roused crowds to their feet. "That was saved for the stage," George explained.

Just months after George joined the Nation of Islam, Sandy gave birth to their second child. As the man of the family, George felt that the children should grow up in a proper Muslim home and helped persuade Sandy to convert to Islam. He quit his sales job at Brownell Electro to direct the NOI's Fish Force. Back in the early 1970s, the Nation had struck a deal with the Peruvian government, which would send boatloads of Pacific whiting to San Francisco. The fish was then transported by NOI freezer trucks to NOI warehouses in Long Island. Not everyone was pleased with the Nation's entrepreneurial spirit. Sometimes the shipments were held up by longshoremen in San Francisco and thousands of dollars' worth of fish became freezer burned. Sometimes the entire cargo would rot. George, like many others, suspected that the mob was behind the sabotage.

Although his new work consumed full days and some evenings, he was little more than a volunteer. Every weekday morning, George reported to work by nine o'clock in a freshly pressed dark suit, black bow tie, and polished black shoes. His official duties as secretary of the Fish Force entailed ordering supplies, divvying out the fish to the sales staff (initially packaged in ten-pound blocks and, later, in more convenient, and realistic, sizes of two or three fish to a box), and recording sales, but he was also expected to hawk Italian ices and fish to passersby.

The fish venture, called Whiting H&G (headed and gutted) never did become profitable. The Nation didn't have the infrastructure to distribute the fish to local markets in Harlem and the Bronx. More importantly, it had no customers. Although the fish sold for well below market average and provided an affordable and nutritious alternative for overcharged locals, people simply did not like this new fish. Even NOI followers did not purchase the whiting, despite the directives and frequent upbraiding from leadership. At the end of a week, all earnings from the flailing business were divided among the minister, the lieutenant, and George. After a year, and a lot of free fish, George had earned only enough money to buy himself another suit.

Other NOI ventures were more successful. By the early 1970s, the NOI had close to a half-million followers and the sympathy of millions more. During these peak years, Elijah Muhammad accumulated an empire worth more than $80 million, including a clothing factory in Chicago, which manufactured official uniforms for NOI followers; a modern printing press; several farms in the South; and a dairy and meat processing plant whose goods were sold in NOI supermarkets and eateries. Bakeries specializing in Shabazz bean pies and whole wheat muffins, meat markets that sold halal beef and poultry, and restaurants that served healthy food like brown rice and carrot fluff, a substitute for mashed potatoes, thrived in many black communities in Boston, Saint Louis, Washington, Chicago, and New York. Some restaurants serving Muslim cuisine became trendy spots to bring a date or to people-watch.

Elijah Muhammad prioritized economic independence for NOI members. All members had to work, and it was preferable to own your own business. Over the years, Black Muslims established hundreds of independent businesses. These included bakeries, gas stations, dry cleaners, cab services, restaurants (outlets for the whiting fish and bean pies), and Steak-N-Takes—take-out restaurants that specialized in sandwiches that were suspiciously similar to the Philly cheesesteak but that came with a special secret sauce and were served on a whole wheat bun.

The Nation's narrative was really America's—a Horatio Alger story—and reinforced the same Protestant ethic of bootstrap capitalism. Still, for many young men like George, Elijah Muhammad's appeal for economic independence delivered hope without substance. They were willing but not able, lacking basic business acumen or practical know-how. George, who still saw himself as an artist, supplemented his meager income by designing signs for NOI ventures, such as the Fish House, at 125th Street and Eighth Avenue, and private Muslim-owned businesses, such as the Steak-n-Take restaurants in Harlem and the Bronx.

The duties and demands of their new faith took a toll on George and Sandy's marriage. Sandy, who had followed George into Islam and had taken the Arabic name Shaheeda, was now teaching elementary school at the University of Islam, located at the refurbished Mosque No. 7 in Harlem. George was spending most of his time at the Bronx mosque, working hard but barely earning enough to get him there and back. At night, when he wasn't attending meetings, he was out selling *Muhammad Speaks* newspapers or drumming up business for his fledgling sign business. With two toddlers at home and a third child on the way, Sandy resented George for not shouldering his financial responsibility and pressured him to get a real job.

At one point, they went to see Minister Farrakhan for marriage counseling. He offered them platitudes and sent them on their way. For a brief time they convinced themselves that Farrakhan's faith in them would see them through, but after the third child was born, they knew Farrakhan had been mistaken. Sandy could no longer work and, despite the NOI taboo on accepting government assistance, George encouraged her to go on welfare. He didn't want to give up his sign business, which he believed was about to take off; a few months of welfare payments just might buy him enough time to prove it to her. She'd have to lie about him living there, he warned her. Although the U.S. Supreme Court had struck down the "man in the house" rule in 1968, penalties remained for intact families (families in which the biological father lived in the home).

Sandy met with the caseworker alone but admitted during the interview that she was married and living with her husband. When she later reported to George that they were ineligible for welfare, he became furious. He was convinced that she had intentionally sabotaged the interview, along with their marriage and his chances of becoming an artist.

Even as George walked out on Sandy and the children, he blamed her for giving up on him. She should have had faith in him, he said. If she hadn't fucked up the interview, he never would have left, and if he hadn't left, he could have pursued his dream, which, he was certain, had been just within his grasp. It wasn't. Although he fantasized about becoming the next William Blake or Picasso, he had been losing his intellectual edge and artistic skills for years. He may even have been remotely aware of the decline, but the admission would have been terrifying.

George moved to a hovel on West 97th Street. He took a full-time security job that just barely paid the rent, and he reined in much of his volunteer work with the Nation. At one point, Sandy asked him to come home, but he was too proud and unforgiving. Eventually she filed for a divorce and remarried as soon as the papers were finalized. Like a woman on the run, she moved with their children to Atlanta, changed her name, severed all ties with George, and swore her friends to silence on her whereabouts. He lost all contact with his children until many years later, when his eldest son, Khalid, searched for him. By that time, George had been diagnosed as manic-depressive and was caught inside a revolving door that led between the insanity of the streets and the insanity of the psychiatric wards.

7

FREE FALL

THE 1970s were a low point in the history of New York and of our family. The city's poverty rate, already 14.8 percent at the start of the decade, soared to 20 percent by 1980—seven points higher than that of the nation. During the same period, more than eight hundred thousand New Yorkers—more than ten percent of the population—deserted the city.

Large chunks of Amsterdam and Columbus Avenues, today posh and coveted, were considered off-limits to all but the most intrepid New Yorkers. As the soldiers returned from Vietnam, the alleyways and subways became littered with heroin addicts. Stumbling but never quite falling, they seemed to defy gravity, as if held off the floor by marionette strings. The subway cars became the canvas for young graffiti artists. Sometimes offensive, sometimes beautiful, their underground art became synonymous with urban cool and rebellion. There was ample time to admire their work; as transit services were slashed, one could stand for an eternity waiting for a local in the off-peak hours. The city's parks had become outdoor bazaars for weed and other drugs—"I got the weed, I got the speed, I got whatever you need." The small park squares, like those at the intersection of 72nd Street and Broadway, were notorious and were dubbed "needle parks." Times

Square was overrun with prostitutes, drug dealers, and hawkers of stolen goods. Rookie cops were sent to patrol the streets; they walked in packs of ten and looked like scared teenagers, too timid to confront the three-ring circus taking place before their eyes.

New York City's infrastructure was crumbling, too, and in 1973, just as the Twin Towers set a new record for the world's tallest buildings, a large section of the West Side Highway collapsed. By 1975, the city was teetering on the edge of bankruptcy, but President Gerald Ford refused to bail it out. Ford's press secretary compared New York to "a wayward daughter hooked on heroin," adding, "You don't give her $100 a day to support her habit." On October 30, the *Daily News* broke the story with the now-famous headline "Ford to City: Drop Dead." Corporations followed government resources out to the suburbs, and middle-class whites followed.

As municipal services were yanked, the streets became thinly policed and criminals enjoyed a new lenience from the courts. The criminal justice system was overtaxed and under-resourced, forcing many prosecutors to drop or reduce charges against felons and encouraging judges to dispense the lightest possible sentences. According to one study conducted in the late 1970s, a mere 4 percent of those arrested for violent crimes spent any time in prison, and only 30 percent of convicted murderers served more than ten years. This, in turn, only emboldened convicts when they returned to the streets.

Meanwhile, the sprawling warehouses and lofts of SoHo—the old industrial area south of Houston Street—became the sites of a new artistic renaissance. Painters, sculptors, musicians, and performance artists rented entire floors to stage their shows. Galleries, bars, restaurants, and boutiques opened soon after, catering to a new bohemia. And as the East Village spilled into Alphabet City, new urban artists negotiated public space with Ukrainians and Hells Angels. For all its grit and anarchy, New

York throbbed with life, energy, and magic at every turn. "No, it was not a decade for the dainty," James Wolcott reminisced, in his ode to the decade. "Experienced awareness of the omnipresence of gunky debris, broken glass, and danger sharpened our reflexes to jungle-cat quickness."

Uptown, in Harlem's valley, schools were underserved and understaffed, and the infant mortality rate far outstripped that of the rest of the city. The community had long suffered from overcrowding, dilapidated housing, and poor health services, but postwar industrial decline, combined with federal policies that shifted billions in taxpayer dollars to build an interstate highway system and research parks in the suburbs, spurred white flight and brought the city and Harlem to its knees. Meanwhile, the continued effects of housing discrimination trapped the black poor in the city.

A century ago, George Haynes Sr. warned of the disastrous effects of segregation: how the very act of creating social closure, of separating groups into different neighborhoods and jobs, would ignite prejudice against them, and that these cutoff spaces would make blacks alien and unknowable and thus less sympathetic to whites. His indictment was as relevant in 1970s Harlem as when he first wrote it, in 1913.

> Crowded into segregated districts; living in poor houses for the most part for which they pay high rentals; often untaught and without teachers in the requirements of town life; walled in by inefficiency, lack of training and the chance to get the training; usually restricted from well-paid occupations by the prejudice of fellow-employees and frequently by the prejudice of employers; with a small income and the resulting low standard of living, the wonder is not that Negroes have a uniformly higher death-rate than whites in the cities and towns, but that the mortality is as small as it is and shows signs of decrease.

Harlem has long sustained a diverse working- and middle-class community, but its image as a hardened, drug- and crime-infested slum has stubbornly endured in the national consciousness. True, it has always had its pockets of extreme poverty, but the extreme poor remain marginalized even within Harlem. When I was growing up, I learned to steer clear of certain blocks, like Fifth Avenue near 126th Street, a known drug spot, where some of the poorest residents lived. And public housing projects elicited the same fear among many Harlemites as Harlem elicited among most downtown New Yorkers. For us, the real slum was somewhere *in* Harlem and not embodied *by* Harlem. Even for those residents within the projects, particular apartments housed the "real" ghetto residents.

By the early 1970s, heroin use had peaked and cocaine was quickly gaining ground. The homicide rate soared as the drug trade flourished. In his 1978 article for *New York* magazine, "Dodge City, The Deadliest Precinct in Town," Randy Young reported on the 32nd Precinct in Harlem, "a square mile of urban badland" where, in just four years, 360 men, women, and children were "shot, knifed, beaten, bludgeoned, or otherwise battered to death." In one year alone, fifty shootings and eighteen murders occurred around a single street corner in the valley—147th Street and Eighth Avenue—as gangs and pushers rivaled for control of the drug trade.

For many Americans, Harlem and the South Bronx were linked with vice and depravity, but, for local residents, it was the rampant police corruption that warranted condemnation. A culture of graft was deeply entrenched throughout the New York City police department, but nowhere did a dirty cop thrive more than in poor black communities like Harlem. As the Knapp Commission report revealed, in 1972, everyone—from the uniformed officers to the drug squad detectives to the supervisors—got a piece of the action. Corruption didn't stop with the police but permeated every level of the criminal justice system; bail bondsmen, defense attorneys, prosecutors, and even certain judges were paid off.

Police malfeasance ranged from keeping the cash or drugs confiscated in drug raids and arrests to protecting dealers—even providing them with armed protection—to actually engaging in narcotics trafficking themselves, selling confiscated drugs to addicts or introducing potential customers to drug dealers. Some officers felt little remorse for plundering a community they held in contempt. Officer William Phillips, who emerged during the commission hearings as one of the most remorseless of these pilferers, described Harlem as "paradise" for a dirty cop. In his 1973 memoir *On the Pad: The Underworld and Its Corrupt Police—Confessions of a Cop on the Take* (written with Leonard Shecter), Phillips laid bare his contempt for the community and its residents. "The whole fucking Harlem stinks. Every hallway smells of piss, garbage, smelly fucking people. I hated the fucking place." (Three years after his book was published, Phillips was sentenced for the 1968 murder of a pimp who failed to pay protection and of the young prostitute who witnessed the killing. He was released on parole in 2007.)

By the mid-1970s, "health food" stores started popping up all over Harlem. These were really undercover weed spots selling dime, nickel, and even three-dollar trade bags of low-grade Mexican. The busiest spot I knew was down on Amsterdam Avenue, between 126th and 127th Streets. The place was lined with bulletproof glass, and only a handful of items appeared on the shelves, obviously just for show. You walked up to the counter, reached through the Plexiglas maze, and dropped your money. The attendant eyed you up and down, checking that you weren't a cop, and then passed a trade bag—a small folded manila envelope—back through the window. Curiously, a squad car always seemed to be parked just down the block. No one from the community was surprised when, some twenty years later, thirty rogue officers of the 30th Precinct were brought down on corruption charges that included conducting illegal raids on drug dealers, stealing drugs and cash, selling protection to drug dealers, and engaging in narcotics trafficking. It turned out that the "Dirty 30" had had a long run siphoning off money in Harlem. As one cop testified during the Mollen Commission hearing, "Police officers view the community as a candy store."

My straight-shooter dad, now in his sixties, was still working as a parole officer in the South Bronx. Sometimes I wondered whether he got his fashion tips from the old cop shows on television, which dressed their detectives in tweed jackets and wingtip shoes. Pop dressed like this every day of his career, a snub-nosed .38 tucked inside his belt line and ready for business, his King Sano pipe tobacco never far from reach. He had a Dick Tracy look about him. Square jawed and square shouldered; a man who could be trusted to do the right thing. A gentleman's officer—cut from the same social cloth as the light-skinned Tuskegee Airmen you might have read about or had the fortune to meet. College educated, well-spoken, and raised with the social expectation to look a white man in the eye and not break his gaze, he was part of a generation of Negro men whose behaviors demanded respect, even from the most begrudging.

Still, although no one at the Division of Parole would have dared to use the word *nigger*—at least not to my father's face— he must have heard it plenty on the job. It was tossed about too liberally among prison guards and on-the-beat cops for him not to have heard it. Walking in on a rant about some "nigger" drug dealer or thug who had broken parole, would he have put his colleagues at ease, making out like he hadn't heard them? Or would he have glared and made them wince? His natural reserve in the face of confrontation, which often infuriated my mother, may actually have augmented his status of superiority and power over them. If so, it was unintentional. He had no pretensions.

Pop took great pride in his work. During the 1970s, when Puerto Ricans and Dominicans made up a larger share of his parolees, he learned Spanish. He bought beginner language tapes, which he labored through at home, and practiced his fledgling skills with us all. "Buenos días señor. Dónde está tu mamá?" His accent was atrocious! Although being a parole officer wasn't what he had set out to do when he was young, he came to love his job, and probably many of his parolees, and he often boasted about never having had to use his gun in all of his thrity-five years on the job.

Pop was an ideal role model for the young men who were making their way back into society. He was squeaky clean and abided by a strict moral code.

Rules were important, not just to keep law and order but also to ensure that everyone got a square deal. He had a folksy side, too, and loved rambling on, to anyone who would listen, about his heyday in the army. To me, none of his stories were particularly telling, or compelling, yet there was something comforting about them. They embodied, or at least conjured, a time when life was simpler, when the lines between good and bad were clear. He was classic Americana.

The New York State Division of Parole office was located at East 161st Street and Morris Avenue, just on the cusp of the South Bronx and down the street from Yankee Stadium. The area had seen a dramatic decline since Pop first reported for duty in the early 1950s. The once thriving community of Jews, Italians, and Irish had long since relocated to the suburbs, having taken advantage of the low-interest federal loans, introduced after the war, which made home ownership possible for millions of Americans. Meanwhile, discriminatory practices in housing kept blacks from following suit. Racially based restrictive covenants, used to prevent Negroes from purchasing houses in white neighborhoods, remained in effect well after the 1948 Supreme Court case of *Shelley v. Kraemer*. The Supreme Court invalidated the

enforcement of racial covenants by the lower courts, but the social practice of restricting black and brown homeownership continued. During the 1950s, new housing developments, built by
entrepreneurs like Abraham Levitt and his sons, transformed
thousands of acres of farmland in New Jersey, Pennsylvania, and
Long Island into tens of thousands of homes for U.S. veterans
and their families. Blacks were barred from purchasing homes
in Levitt-built communities as well as in hundreds, if not thousands of other planned communities throughout America.

After decades of white flight and deindustrialization, the
South Bronx had earned its standing as one of the worst slums in
America. It had the further distinction of claiming the highest
unsolved homicide rate in the country. "The Bronx is burning"
became a familiar refrain in the 1970s. Tenants routinely set fire
to their own apartments so that they could be relocated to better
public housing projects and collect up to $3,000 in compensation.
Landlords, too, participated in the scam, hiring professional
"torchers" to gut buildings that were no longer profitable and then
filing hefty insurance claims. Whatever could be salvaged from
the buildings—copper pipes, fixtures—was filched by junkies. The
number of standing housing units in the South Bronx dropped
from 55,400 in 1970 to 36,100 in 1980.

The population plummeted during this period, as well, from
247,000 to 91,800. All but the poorest of the poor fled the area.
With a total collapse of civil order, gangs moved into the vacuum
and created their own social order. The first reports of gangs in
the South Bronx came in 1970. By the end of the year, at least
fifteen gangs had been established and countless more would join
the ranks over the decade. The Black Pearls, the Black Spades,
the Immortals, the Turbans, the Savage Skulls, and the Savage
Nomads were among the most notorious. They were violent and
heavily armed and, despite their claims of antidrug vigilantism,
many cashed in on the lucrative drug trade.

While conditions up on Sugar Hill also declined during this time, some black professionals, and even a few consulates, began gentrifying our neighborhood. Mr. Hayes, a retired New York City school principal and amateur Egyptologist, moved in next door and renovated the former rooming house, pipe by pipe. Hayes was the quintessential new Harlemite: educated, well-traveled, and unapologetically Afrocentric. He towered at six foot four and carried himself as though he were the descendant of kings. He was soon joined by Mr. Bey, a local entrepreneur and sometime vendor, who took over a brownstone across the street. Bey stood about six foot one, and his long dreadlocks were peppered with grey. He might have been in his fifties but he had a lean boxer's physique and a bearing that let a person know that, if he was looking for a place to shoot drugs or sleep them off, he should look elsewhere. They, along with other new residents, stood vigil over the block, replacing the "old heads" like my father.

The pride these newcomers took in their homes underscored my father's negligence. I wondered whether Pop secretly wished that the house would collapse, as if it were a reminder of the love that his father, and now Daisy, withheld from him. Her refusal to tend to the house epitomized her lack of concern for him. Pop, in turn, withheld money for the house's upkeep. The chaos crept up on them, and they took on every new challenge in stride. One year, it was the kitchen cabinets that they learned to do without; the next year, the kitchen sink. A long string of adjustments that they made together, as a team.

❤

Convent Avenue remained fairly stable through the 1970s, but right around the corner from our house—on Saint Nicholas Avenue, between 145th and 146th Streets—a big-time coke dealer

122 ◼ FREE FALL

held sway, operating out of a local bar called the Mark 4. He must have been stuck up a dozen times before moving his operation to 147th Street, between Broadway and Amsterdam, one of the roughest blocks in the neighborhood. I became well acquainted with the block during the summer of 1975, when I took a job with the Washington Heights/West Inwood Community Mental Health Center, up on Amsterdam Avenue. Unique for its time, the center was a truly community-based, community-run venture, with a board made up entirely of neighborhood residents—including both of my parents.

My mother was good friends with Emma Bowen, a fiery community activist and major player in the mental health field. Bowen had been appointed, under Mayor John Lindsay, as executive secretary of the New York City Mental Health, Mental Retardation and Alcoholism Services. She would go on to found the Upper Manhattan Mental Health Center, as well as Black Citizens for a Fair Media and the Foundation for Minority Interest in Media. My mother had always had a knack for befriending powerful women. She was poised and sophisticated and demonstrated none of the hard, blind ambition that might have threatened women less secure. She never surpassed or encroached. She excelled in the role of second-in-command and never strove to be anything else. Her connections to Emma Bowen were instrumental during my interview with the Community Mental Health Center; I was immediately placed as an intern in the public relations office and made supervisor, at fifteen years old, of two kids even younger than me.

Our job was to provide outreach to the community. Despite the wealth of resources and services that the center offered, it had a real image problem. The building, a high-tech monstrosity, stuck out like a sore thumb. It was set back from the street in mini-plaza fashion and seemed alien and removed from the community in every way. And, with its spiffy professionals scurrying through the revolving doors, it had a distinctly bourgeois undertone.

We pounded the sidewalks that summer, hitting every single building in the catchment area—from 155th Street and Riverside Drive to 125th Street and Amsterdam, and then reaching well into the valley, to 120th and Saint Nicholas Avenue. Armed with our flyers, we rang doorbells and stopped people in their hallways, on their stoops, and in the streets. Flyers were unusual in Harlem, save for the occasional Chinese menus dropped off in bulk in building lobbies, and outsiders never dared to make direct contact with the residents. Yet the point of our job was to connect to the community. People were much more likely to read the literature and ask questions if we handed it to them directly.

Some of the scariest blocks we passed through that summer were the ones in my own neighborhood. The high 140s, between Amsterdam and Broadway, were particularly dicey. I knew these streets from my days in public school—my two best friends had lived on those blocks—and from my childhood trips to the laundromat with Pop. The buildings were mostly old tenement walk-ups. There was piss on the stairs and busted glass at the entries, where young thugs chilled and hassled passersby. If you happened to be an outsider—white or black—especially one distributing flyers, you were likely in for an ass whipping. I honed my New York savvy on the job, that hard-boiled sixth sense needed to size someone up in an instant. I learned who to stop for and who to brace for. A smile, a nod, or a request as innocent as the time of day had to be weighed with breakneck speed and military precision. You're asking for the time, but what do you really want? Is this a mugging? And in the 1970s, when even petty thieves carried knives or guns, a mugging could be fatal.

My brother Alan had learned this a few summers before, after stopping at a check cashing storefront. A couple of thugs watched as he placed the bills in his wallet and the wallet into the left pocket of his jeans. As he exited the building, they stepped out in front of him, one brandishing a small knife, the other a machete. His whole body was shaking when he got home that night, and he could barely vocalize what had happened. Not that it needed much explaining. His jeans were shredded from top to bottom; a hole gaped in the left pocket, where his wallet had once sat. Amazingly, not a single hair on his body had been grazed.

It never occurred to my parents to move to a safer neighborhood. The rising crime meant only that we needed to adjust our behavior—a stance that many die-hard New Yorkers took during the 1970s. We learned to carry any serious cash in our sock and to put a few bucks in our pocket for the privilege of walking the streets. We called that "mugging money." You didn't want to be mugged with nothing in your pocket; after all of the effort it took for a mugger to single you out and follow you, not to mention the risk he was taking to pull out a knife or a gun, it was best to make it worth his while. "Here's five dollars, a little something for your troubles, and thank you for not knifing me."

Not everyone in our neighborhood chose to stay. Some middle-class blacks fled to quiet communities in Queens, like Hollis, Saint Albans, or Cambria Heights; others followed the buzz to Co-op City, the gigantic new cooperative housing development in the Bronx. A few residents even returned to the South. By the 1980s, when our home became truly dysfunctional and the neighborhood was overrun with guns and drug dealers, Daisy did entertain fantasies of moving to a swanky doorman building downtown. She identified with George and Louise—the affluent black couple from the television sitcom *The Jeffersons*, who moved to a "dee-luxe apartment in the sky"—and she set her sights on a new high-rise co-op development on 96th Street and Broadway, just down the street from her favorite restaurant, Empire Szechuan. But by then it was too late; Pop was nearing retirement, the house was paid off, and he wouldn't consider taking out another mortgage.

◆

By the mid-1970s, the shape of our lives was solidifying. Alan had eloped with his high school English tutor, Marcia, and now was studying music at Bronx Community College. They married before the ink on his diploma had dried. She was twenty-eight, he eighteen. She was white, Jewish, five feet tall, and ever so plump. He was six foot two—although his bushy Afro added another few inches—and wiry. When they stood side by side, they made an Abbott and Costello silhouette.

When Alan turned twenty-one, he used his inheritance from our grandfather to buy a small two-story house in Yonkers, on the aptly named Valentine Lane. I had an open invitation and spent many weekends with them, as much to be with my big brother as to escape the insanity at home. While Marcia took care of all the "grownup" stuff, like cooking and cleaning, Alan and I got to be big kids, playing with remote control tanks, riding bikes, and listening to music—Procol Harum, Tower of Power, Carlos Santana, Blind Faith, the Allman Brothers and, of course, Hendrix. His icons became mine. His vices, too. He turned me on to cannabis, bringing out a custom-made wooden pipe, a small, eight-inch-square box that contained rolling papers, and two small piles—one containing seeds and stems, the other some fresh crumbled bits of dark, condensed Jamaican lambsbread herb. He figured I'd come across it sooner or later and wanted me to know what the real thing was.

I took on many of Alan's habits and mannerisms. At fifteen, I started smoking his cigarettes—Nat Sherman King Size Filtered Cigarettellos, wrapped in unbleached brown and slightly sweet Maduro paper. They were natural, sophisticated, and exclusive.

Like us! I began leaving open the top two buttons of my sports shirts and rolling up the sleeves; a bandana hung from my back pocket, just like Alan. I started thinking of myself as taller, leaner. I added a little bop to my walk, my cap cocked just so to the side. To complete my look, I wore a long, single-breasted wool overcoat from Saks. It fit perfectly with the self-consciously-cool-kid-from-Harlem image that I had fashioned for myself at private school.

I was now at Dwight, a Jewish prep school then located on the fashionable East Side. Emerson was a feeder school for two high schools: the Dwight School and Columbia Grammar. Dwight was good but second-tier. The smarter kids went to Columbia Grammar. I had never been an A student or particularly ambitious. My grades were good, but not great, and that's how I saw myself. Still, it came as a blow when I learned that I wouldn't be going on with my friends. I never saw much of them after that. I think there was a whole status thing about the kids who went off to Columbia Grammar.

At Dwight, I entered the world of New York's preparatory elite, where the children of the super rich and the children of the merely rich mixed. The parents included comedian Rodney Dangerfield; Italian jeweler Mario Buccellati; advertising executive Jerry Della Femina, who founded the eponymous agency and whose memoir would later be the inspiration for *Mad Men*; and music mogul Dee Anthony, who represented Tony Bennett, Ian Anderson (of Jethro Tull), and Joe Cocker. One room in the Anthonys' apartment was lined with platinum and gold records. I was one of two black kids in my grade, which gave me a status of sorts. The only time I heard the N-word was when a boy who had a crush on a pretty blond girl I was dating questioned why she'd want to date a nigger. The comment still smarts today.

My teachers were overwhelmingly encouraging, although a few singled me out as a problem kid. The first was my seventh-grade science teacher, Mr. Latundra. He used to keep a six-foot-long boa constrictor in the science lab, and many of us called him a sadist. He'd grab you by the arm and give you pressure pinches. Once he grabbed me by the throat. And then there was Mr. Myers, who taught American history and debate and coached mini-junior varsity soccer and basketball. Every once in a while you meet someone who takes a strong dislike to you, and you know they'll do anything they can to crush you. I knew early on that Mr. Myers was one of those people. While Mr. Latundra was brutish, Mr. Myers was conniving, supercilious, and a little bit effeminate. All the kids called him a faggot, in the days when nobody thought twice about wielding that word as a weapon. And we weren't shy about letting him hear it. I was as boorish as the rest of them but, unlike my classmates, I feared Mr. Myers. Maybe I knew he could hurt me more.

Mr. Myers used a recitation style of learning essays, in which we'd break the essay into its component parts, memorize and recite each chunk, and then string them all together. It was rote learning, yes, but it taught us structure and sequence and gave us the building blocks to write compelling essays of our own. In many ways, he was a tremendous teacher. Yet he had a cruel streak.

Once, in debate class, the question of interracial dating came up, and he said that he couldn't conceive of ever dating a black woman. Most of the kids thought it was a strange comment, because they doubted he'd ever date any woman—black or white—but the fact that he had to make it public, and that I was the only black kid in the class, made his comment seem personal. In eighth grade American history, we had a lesson on slavery. Mr. Myers told me to stand during his lecture. It was mortifying, as if I were being cast back on an auction block for that moment. Everyone looked, some appearing to be as embarrassed for me as I was for myself.

Our day of reckoning came that spring, during the lower-school basketball championship. At the time, there was an intense rivalry between me and Victor, a weird kid from the ghetto who claimed to have a basketball court at his house. We were in the last minutes of the game, with a two-point lead over Victor's team. I made a steal and was heading down the court for a sure basket when someone slammed me into the wall. I fell to the floor and looked up to see Victor streaking toward the basket for an uncontested layup. I was sure the referee, Mr. Myers, was going to call a foul. Instead, he stood over me with a big mocking grin that said he knew there had been a foul but wasn't going to call it. My sense of justice knocked all common sense aside. I got to my feet, looked up at him—I was five four and he was close to five ten—and called him a faggot. Then I slapped him across the face. I did it without thinking, although I realize now that a public slapping was far more humiliating than any punch could have been. He looked at me with disbelief. After a long silence, he blew his whistle and gave me a technical foul. Then I took off my shirt and threw it at him.

The gym went wild, and Mr. Myers ended the game abruptly, heading off to fetch Mr. Spahn, the headmaster. I was summoned to the office and told that I would be expelled and that my parents must report to school that next morning. I was less fearful of being expelled than of disappointing my parents, but when I told them what I'd done, they were remarkably supportive. They knew that I had always been well liked by my teachers and had earned good citizenship commendations since first grade. And they'd been paying close attention to my mounting grievances against Mr. Myers over the past months—the book he hurled at me from across the table, his request that I stand during his lecture on slavery. Just a few days earlier, I'd sworn that I would strike back if he kept taunting me, and although they had warned me that this would be a disastrous move, here they were now, in total support.

Support also came from my classmates, and even a few teachers. My seventh-grade English teacher, Mrs. Schwartz, approached me the next morning and whispered in my ear, "You should have kicked him in the balls." The headmaster was less sympathetic. When my parents and I were brought into his office, it became clear that he and Myers had prepared a little show for us. Spahn set the stage, describing, in a grave tone, a "most serious situation," in which a faculty member had been injured. Then Myers entered the room, cupping his fragile face in his hand. My mother was appalled that a grown man would feign injury from a slap dealt more than twelve hours earlier by a scrawny runt like me. She went on the attack, citing all the incidents of abuse that I had suffered from Mr. Myers. And although she never explicitly threatened a lawsuit, it was made clear to Mr. Spahn that expulsion was not an option unless he wanted to go to court. To save face, Mr. Spahn decreed that I would be formally expelled for two weeks—the length of spring vacation—and that if I agreed to apologize to the entire lower school, there would be no permanent record of the incident. I told him no, that I'd only agree to apologize to my class. Surprisingly, he relented.

As the years progressed, I enjoyed a new independence from my family, spending weekends and holidays at the homes of my friends from Dwight. I became acquainted with some of the most exclusive addresses in Manhattan—Beekman Place, Sutton Place, Park Avenue, Fifth Avenue, and the grand prewar apartments of the Upper West Side. Summer homes on Fire Island. Country homes upstate or in the Hamptons. My mother was out quite a bit herself, "gallivanting," as my father called it, with her artist friends—and with one musician friend in particular. (Years later, her best friend would confide that she'd been having an affair with him all along.) Having sold the last of the properties inherited from his father, Pop was now borrowing to keep me in private school. He grew ever more tightfisted about money and suspended even token maintenance work on the house.

George, on the other hand, was feeling flush. Flush with pocket change and potential. The minimum-wage security job he'd taken when he left Sandy—working the graveyard shift at construction sites throughout the city—had grown into a comfy office job at company headquarters out in Long Island City. He was a manager now, earning close to $240 a week, but it was still barely enough to make ends meet in the city.

By now, he had left the Nation of Islam. The Honorable Elijah Muhammad had died in 1975, and the sweeping changes that his son, Wallace D. Muhammad, brought to the Nation—steering its followers away from a separatist, race-based theology and toward the orthodox teachings of Sunni Islam—did not resonate with George. Gone were the pomp and the pride of blackness. Gone were the fervent rhetoric and the certainty that came with it. The black Islam that George had known, rooted in esoteric precepts and catechisms, no longer existed. The Supreme Wisdom Lessons that he had mastered no longer needed to be remembered, and the answers he had memorized and took great pride in reciting were to questions that no longer mattered. The path he had at last found turned out to lead nowhere.

By the time Louis Farrakhan revived the remnants of the old Nation, six years later, George had chosen a different path. It began in the bars of midtown Manhattan and meandered a hundred blocks north into Harlem. Bars offered some of the solace he had found at the mosque—a space for the spirit to soar, for a smile of recognition when you walked through the door, bestowing an instant sense of community.

The entrepreneurial spirit that had been instilled in him by the Nation was still alive. He was hatching a business plan, on the periphery of show business, with a few of his old mosque brothers, ex-NOIers like himself who never made the shift to Sunni Islam. These were the early days of cable television, and the field was wide open. With no content regulations, no experience needed, and no talent required, a cacophony of content sputtered across the airwaves. The Boy Scouts of America were followed by the dominatrix Fran Beck. Anarchists and erotic artists, psychics and crank callers, puppets and militants, church choirs and smut peddlers all had a voice in this new electronic democracy. Yet, with only two channels available to the public—channels C and D—access to free airtime was at a premium. (The term *public* is relative here because, in the early days of cable television, access was limited to the more moneyed neighborhoods of Manhattan. In Harlem, we waited for years to get cable access, and some folks were still waiting as late as 1989, when Harlem would finally become fully wired.)

A third channel was added in 1976. Channel J was the world's first leased access channel, and for just fifty dollars anyone could purchase an hour of airtime. Whatever flimsy veneer of propriety there was left to break through, it was penetrated by Channel J. Over the years, it titillated audiences with such classics as *The Ugly George Hour*, a precursor to *Girls Gone Wild*, in which the bizarre George Urban, clad in a silver lamé jumpsuit or an open vest and short shorts, roamed the city in search of women who would agree to expose their breasts for his camera; *The Robin Byrd Show*, featuring stripper and porn star Robin Cohen; *Interludes After Midnight*, a nude talk show for swingers; and *Midnight Blue*, produced by *Screw* magazine publisher Al Goldstein.

In this pre-YouTube universe, anyone could be a star and, as George and his associates surmised, many didn't mind paying for a few minutes of spotlight. His group came up with the scheme of producing a talent show in which the talent paid to appear on the show. What made the plan so appealing was that one of the partners was named William Morris—not *the* William

Morris, the talent agent, but if no one asked, they'd be none the wiser. Taking full advantage of the coincidence, they named the program *The William Morris Show* and put out ads in *Variety* and *Backstage* magazines: "William Morris seeking talent!" Eventually the William Morris Agency threatened to sue them if they didn't stop using the name.

For auditions they rented space at the Ansonia—the grand Beaux-Arts residential hotel on Broadway and 73rd Street that had once been home to Igor Stravinsky, Sergei Rachmaninoff, Enrico Caruso, Jack Dempsey, and Babe Ruth, as well as to the "Policy King," Al Adams, who had moved to the Ansonia fresh from a stint at Sing Sing. The Ansonia oozed opulence and extravagance, with its wedding cake facade, its outrageous size—fifty thousand square feet—and its sumptuous interiors, which included Turkish baths, a lavish fountain with live seals, and the world's largest indoor swimming pool. By now, the hotel was in bad disrepair, and the defunct baths and pool had been transformed into a gay bathhouse, complete with a discotheque and cabaret, an orgy room, and a candy machine that dispensed K-Y Jelly. A young Bette Midler (known then as Bathhouse Betty) launched her career there. In 1977, the bathhouse changed hands again, morphing into the notorious swinger's club Plato's Retreat.

The William Morris Show's production team—some twelve men and women—formed a club, which met at a disco out in Brooklyn that was owned and operated by one of the associates. William Morris and his main sidekick, Alton, were considered the leaders of the club and the show's head producers. They emceed the show and told jokes between performances. What George brought to the team was experience in managing money. In his former days as secretary of his mosque, he had kept an ongoing record of finances. This was a great asset to the club, which lacked some of the harder skills. With his Horace Mann education, he was also among the more articulate members of the group. Thus, George served as the group's bookkeeper and also handled the public relations, a responsibility that involved making the nightly rounds of trendy bars and clubs to scout talent, recruit singers and dancers to audition, drum up interest in the show, and maybe even get the ear of a big-time television producer.

Alcohol was free flowing in the seventies, and every bar had a happy hour to draw in the after-work crowd. Some started as early as four o'clock, and it wasn't uncommon to see folks stumbling to their cars at five in the afternoon. If customers lingered long enough, they could get a free meal, too—standard buffet fare, but enough to keep them occupied for an hour or two until the night crowd started showing up. Back then, bars stayed open until the bartender called it quits. And then there were the illegal after-hours spots, which welcomed the dawn of a new day. George knew them all. He hit the big downtown hotels, the jazz dens on upper Amsterdam and Columbus Avenues, and his old Harlem standbys, like the Red Rooster, Club Barron, Smalls Paradise, and Count Basie's Lounge—a plush little restaurant and bar where he had first taken Sandy.

He didn't mind the occasional late hours at his day job. Before signing off from work, he'd reach into the metal cabinet where he kept his personal life out of sight and slip into his party attire. Mom was still buying his clothes—trendy double-knit slacks and Qiana shirts from Saks that belied his modest salary and honed his new image as a rising television producer and talent agent.

The late hours and booze took their toll the next day; it became harder to make it to work on time, and no amount of coffee could yank him from his morning stupor. One night, he was turned on to Sweet Pea, a dealer and part-time pimp who sometimes operated out of the men's bathroom at Mikell's, a jazz and neo-soul club down on Columbus Avenue. Sweet Pea lived in the Times Square Motor Hotel, a run-down single-room-occupancy hotel on 43rd Street, off Eighth Avenue, that was home to pimps and prostitutes of a certain ilk. Although Sweet Pea carried himself like a big man, he was all of five foot three, and his platform shoes—pushing up the hem of his pants legs, exposing the little bulge of his calves—only magnified his small stature. Another unfortunate antic was that, while everybody else used the little four-inch red straws for sniffing lines of cocaine, Sweet Pea opted for a full-size straw—a big straw for a big man—except that the powder dotted his walrus mustache like snowcapped candies, turning it literally into "nose candy."

That night, George bought his first dime piece, which he easily made stretch through the week, using it as a little perk-me-up in the morning to cushion the hangover and jolt him into daylight. Nothing he couldn't handle, and so he handled it every day, week after week. Eventually he would need bigger jolts, but by then he and Sweet Pea had entered into an understanding.

One day, Sweet Pea asked George to lend him forty dollars to pick up a package. George had no illusions about the "package," nor did he care. Sweet Pea was good for the money. When it came time to settle, though, Sweet Pea whipped out a fat plastic bag and doled out the equivalent of forty dollars in coke. What George would later learn was that forty dollars of dealer-quality cocaine, once cut, was worth at least eighty dollars on the street. Soon, George was bankrolling Sweet Pea on a regular basis, each month handing over a few hundred dollars, which Sweet Pea would repay in kind. And so it was that George's cocaine use grew in direct proportion to his own generosity.

There was no end to George's usefulness. His access to cable television could help Sweet Pea find women to pimp. In clubs, Sweet Pea would incorporate George into his hustle—"Hey, you want to meet a TV producer?"—giving him instant leverage with the girls. George, in turn, could steer women auditioning for the

show to Sweet Pea, who had other ways of giving them the spotlight they craved. "I got a gig for you!" The next thing you know,
she's standing naked in front of a mechanical screen as it rises
for twenty-five cents. Meanwhile, Sweet Pea gets a finder's fee,
skimmed off the top of her salary by the mob running the house.

"There was this one time," George said, "where Sweet Pea
recruited this girl to work in a peep booth on salary. She had the
overnight shift, and I, believe it or not, had to play babysitter for
her kid and still go to work the next morning. It seems funny
now that I was nervous about being late."

As George's habit outpaced his earnings, he looked to other
sources of income. He had built trust with Sweet Pea by now
and was learning the nuts and bolts of the business, like how to
cut—or double the volume of—cocaine by adding a filler like
benzocaine, otherwise known as "coco snow." So when Sweet
Pea offered to make him a partner, George didn't think twice.

The first thing he did was to invest in a new wardrobe, one
more befitting his new identity He headed over to the Upper
West Side, where Mr. Fowad, the Egyptian owner of a small
discount clothing store, decked him out in pimp splendor: glossy
three-piece suits and matching Stetson hats. To complete the
look, George bought a jar of Nile pomade and slicked his hair
back. Our grandfather was surely turning in his grave! George
even took on a nickname—Dr. G—a good name for a gangster,
he thought. Doctor of healing or of breaking bones.

He began playing the heavy on Sweet Pea's nightly excur-
sions, standing off to the side in his blue suede suit and cocked
blue Stetson, stealing a stance from the Fruit of Islam, while
Sweet Pea made a deal. He got a kick out of seeing the intimi-
dation he could induce, " 'cause it was all a bluff." He told of one
night when he and Sweet Pea were closing a deal outside an after-
hours spot on West 50th Street: "Now, I stood directly behind
the buyer, looking all mean, you know, and Sweet Pea says, 'This

is Dr. G,' in a real serious tone, you know. And then . . . I'm nervous too, you know, but the poor guy says to Sweet Pea, 'Would you ask Dr. G not to stand over me, please?' He was too scared to ask me directly!"

Coke was an elixir that opened magic doors. "It was great for getting into the clubs," George reminisced. "In fact, it was better than money. It was like having a diamond you could smoke." There was a whole cult wrapped up with cocaine. Users grew one long pinkie nail and wore coke spoons around their necks as jewelry. They carried their coke in hundred-dollar bills to show off.

George's day job, once the backbone of his relationship with Sweet Pea, was becoming obsolete. Dealing meant access to real money. Money, power, and women. Still, most of the women George dated had no idea he was dealing coke, or even using it. He tended to go for good girls, like Barbara, a culinary arts student at Hunter College, who worked part time for Tavern on the Green, or Dedjet, the nun turned belly dancer. And then there was Charlotte, another Catholic girl, who shared George's love for jazz. They'd go down to the Village to hear a set of Mingus or Rahsaan Roland Kirk, and, after taking her home, he'd head straight back to the clubs, free to now drink the way he wanted or to do a few lines of coke.

George and Sweet Pea continued to use the "television producer" angle to get into the better-class clubs, where rope lines kept out the riffraff and the nobodies. But not all establishments were so hoity-toity. They covered the pimp and hustler bars, the whorehouses, and the peep show parlors on 42nd Street and along Eighth Avenue. There were the video peep shows, which featured everything from Swedish erotica in the front of the store to—for those who dared to follow the neon arrows to the back— kiddie porn or acts of bestiality involving horses, Great Danes, cows, hens, pigs, or even eels. There were also the live peep shows, where naked girls rotated on a revolving drum and were paid for like parking meters; each time you dropped a quarter, you got a thirty-second peep. Glass partitions separated the girls from the voyeurs but, for a brief period in 1978, the partitions came down, allowing patrons to haggle with the dancers for a more intimate experience.

Despite the enormous profits to be made in adult entertainment, the girls themselves were scraping by. George knew one girl who was only breaking $170 for a thirty-hour week. Still, he reasoned, the conditions beat the streets; the girls were protected, and the premises were kept relatively clean. George recalled the constant cleaning of the booths, the bleaching and mopping of the floors and walls. "You always saw a guy with a mop."

The road from the righteous Nation of Islam to the shadowy underworld of Times Square seems an unlikely one, but both were veiled in mystery and immersed George in a world in which he ceased to exist. George 78X or Dr. G—anyone but George Edmund Haynes III.

That fourth day of August 1976 started out like any other. Alan left his Yonkers home around ten in the morning and biked to Eddie's Bike Shop, at 181st Street and Jerome Avenue in the Bronx, where he worked part time as chief bike mechanic. The distance was only five or six miles, but it was a world apart. Eddie's was in the Morris Heights section of the Bronx, home to one of the most impoverished communities in the city, if not the nation, and gripped by the same destructive forces plaguing the nearby South Bronx—drugs, guns, gangs, and arson. Still, Jerome Avenue was a busy commercial thoroughfare, canopied by the elevated Interborough Rapid Transit line. Alan had brought all of his notebooks with him that day so he could head straight to class after work. He was in his last semester at Bronx Community College and only a few classes away from an associate's degree in music—a milestone for a kid who had always struggled at school. He was twenty-three years old and life was beautiful.

No one knows exactly how he was shot, or even why. Not that any reason could ever be reason enough. That day, local folks had been lining up outside the tiny shop. James, who'd been around for as long as anyone could remember, was in charge of the door. He was only about fifteen but big for his age, especially with his four-inch Afro. At some point, there was a commotion at the front of the store. Alan, who was working in the back, heard shouts and came out to see what was happening. James was arguing with a couple of hoodlums who'd balked at waiting their turn outdoors in the afternoon heat. Words were exchanged, voices raised. The large German shepherd, perched like a sentry in the store window, barked loudly. The manager quickly stepped in and assumed control. Then, briefly, work returned to normal. Sometime later, though, James spotted the thugs outside the store, this time holding a suspicious-looking paper bag. The police were called but, by the time a patrol car arrived, the men had disappeared. The incident was soon forgotten, so when, later that evening, Alan took the dog out for its evening walk, no one gave the incident a second thought. Minutes later, the dog was heard yelping under the El.

The blot from the single pistol shot—a small .25 caliber—was still on Alan's shirt when the police arrived, and a scent, like a spent firecracker, lingered. The shirt was nondescript, a casual cotton variety you could find in any Army Navy store in Manhattan or the Bronx for ten bucks. Blood along the sidewalk soaked the cigarette butts and streamed into the gutter to join the broken glass and bottle caps as Alan spat blood and faded in and out of consciousness.

I've often imagined those last seconds. Was he in pain? Did he ask, *Why me?* Did he try to cry out, "Hey! Does anyone hear me?" although his words couldn't have bubbled through the blood and mucous. Did he hear the No. 4 bus rumble by in his last seconds? James couldn't get the blood off the shepherd's paws for days after.

The night I learned that Alan died, I was camping over at a friend's house. It was after eleven o'clock when my mother placed one of her "emergency" calls. These were the days before call-waiting, when you could get the operator to interrupt a phone call in the event of an emergency. Daisy, who believed that anything blocking her way to her sons was an emergency, used the service liberally, so it didn't seem unusual when my friend's mother was shooed off the phone by the operator and instructed to have me call home.

The second I heard my mother's voice, though, I knew the emergency was real. Her voice was high and tight and she seemed out of breath. She had to say it twice so that I could absorb the words: "Alan has been killed." She told me I didn't have to come home if I didn't want to. And I didn't want to. I relied on my friends to get me through the night. I never asked myself who was there to get my parents through it.

Pop said he didn't need me to go to the morgue with him to identify Alan's body, but he was visibly relieved when I insisted. I can still see Mommy in her housecoat as we walked out the door. Imagining that, any minute, we'd see Alan turning the corner, waving, shouting, "Hey! Everything's OK." The odd calm and stillness of the train, as if the whole world had been put on mute. Getting off at West 23rd Street, walking wordlessly with Pop. The long, numbing stretch of time and crosstown space. The mortuary division of the Department of Hospitals, through which tens of thousands of bodies pass each year. Descending a narrow concrete staircase, standing outside a white door, holding our breath as it opened—just wide enough to let a gurney through.

Alan. There was your face. *I used to curl up in your lap.* There was your nose, your eyes, your ears. *You let me ride on your shoulders when I was a kid.* There was your blue-jean shirt with bloodstains. *You wanted to be Jimmy Hendrix and I wanted to be you.*

We never used the word *murder*. Eventually, we stopped speaking Alan's name altogether. My mother stopped working for a year and began to drink regularly. Pop lingered in the shadows, powerless and uncertain. George stayed missing in action. And I stayed away as much as I could. For a while I kept trekking out to Yonkers, visiting Alan's wife, Marcia, at their house on Valentine Lane, until she became sick with cancer and moved back home to California to die. Her parents, who had rejected Alan and our family from the start, sent a final courtesy call informing us of her passing.

With Marcia gone, I started spending more time at my friends' homes. When I did come home, I spent most of my time on the first floor, taking over the rooms in which the tenants had once lived and that George and Alan later occupied. I painted the rooms, cleaned them ritualistically, and played rock and roll at full blast to drown out the yelling and screaming of my parents. I was developing an ulcer at sixteen and was put on the prescription drug cimetidine for the next two years.

For years, I smoked Nat Shermans, listened to Alan's music, and even took up the bass guitar. Eventually I moved to Yonkers and rented an apartment just a block from where he and Marcia had lived. I saw random events as signs that he was watching over me. These began after Alan visited me in a dream—a dream in which I woke from a dream to find him sitting right beside me. I was so happy, and I cried out, "Hey! Where have you been?" He said he had had to go away but that I shouldn't worry about him. "Everything is all right," he assured me. When I woke, I expected him to be sitting there still, as if time had stood still. After that, I began noticing that the streetlights often burned out just as I passed beneath them. I wasn't the kind of person who believed in the supernatural, yet I couldn't ignore these odd little blips that seemed to say that Alan had found a way to send signals, telling me that he was still watching over me. They continue to this day.

8

MOVING ON DOWN

MY mother kept calling me Alan. Pop and I would freeze until she corrected herself, and then we would carry on as if nothing had happened. Other than these slip-ups, which became less frequent as the year inched forward, his name was never mentioned.

My parents retreated to their own worlds, and they gave me the freedom and the money—despite Pop's protests, my mother raised my weekly allowance to thirty-five dollars—to find my way alone. I spent the money on pizza, movies, weed, and alcohol. My friends and I frequented the old-timer Irish bars and downtown rock-and-roll clubs, many of which catered, after dark, to the underage prep school crowd, and to the many neighborhood discos popping up on the Upper East Side. Our IDs, which we filched from the school office—cheap cardboard squares embossed with the school logo and with blank spaces to type in our names and birthdates—were approved with a wink and a nod.

In grade ten, I began experimenting with psychedelics. My friends and I prepared for our first acid trip like it was a final exam. We read *Be Here Now*, by Ram Dass, and *The Psychedelic Experience: A Manual Based on the Tibetan Book of the Dead*, by

Timothy Leary. And, because Leary told us to, we also read *The Tibetan Book of the Dead*. On the day of our trip, the city was besieged by a blizzard. We claimed the giant avenues of Park and Madison and Fifth for ourselves and trekked into Central Park, where we made fresh tracks in the snow. Our eyes had become magnifying glasses, and we saw God everywhere.

That oneness dissolved as soon as my body and mind reunited and I reclaimed my tiny space.

I joined the literary club at school that year and wrote poems about poverty, police brutality, freedom, and Alan. I inherited $15,000 from Alan's death—Marcia had split the payout from his life insurance with me—and used it to buy all of the things that had had meaning for Alan. I spent the first $3,000 to buy Alan's Guild bass guitar and Sunn amplifier from Marcia, and another five hundred at Crazy Eddie's, one of the earliest discount electronics stores in Manhattan, where I bought my first stereo: a thirty-watt Marantz receiver, a Technics direct-drive turntable with pitch control, and two titanic Cerwin-Vega speakers that could handle two hundred watts of power. I spent the rest of Alan's money slowly and reluctantly, and it lasted well into my midtwenties.

By seventeen, I was becoming more aware that the world was responding to me differently. Women on the subway clutched their purses a little more tightly when I approached. The police watched me more intently. Parents of girls I had known for years—some since third grade—found me less adorable. I was no longer that cute little black boy. I was becoming a young black man, something to be feared. I had fooled myself for years, believing that people—white people—would grow more comfortable with me as I spent more time around them. It was the opposite. The more time I spent, the bigger I got, and the more of a threat I presented.

I saw more of George during this time. Despite his growing cocaine habit, he was still a handsome man and took great care in his appearance. His hair was cropped short, his sideburns neatly trimmed. He was even gaining a little girth. He always looked sharp, thanks to the fancy sweaters and corduroy pants from Saks that Mom continued to dress him in.

By the late 1970s, he had cut his ties with Sweat Pea, who was "snorting up our profits," and was running his own operation. He was a small-time dealer, moving an ounce of coke a week. Cut four times, his profit was $240—about what he had been making at his old security job. His experience was typical of low-level drug dealers. In a 2000 study on drug-dealing gangs, the economist Steven D. Levitt and sociologist Sudhir Venkatesh found earnings to be "enormously skewed," with street-level sellers making roughly the minimum wage. Only a few at the top of the pyramid ever got rich, as Levitt later showed in a chapter from his bestseller *Freakonomics*, "Why Do Drug Dealers Still Live with their Moms?" George's own story was a case in point; before the year was up, he would in fact move back home to Convent Avenue.

He used the first-floor parlor—his old Studio Nefertiti—for the business of cutting coke. By now, he was securing most of his supply from the Cubans and Dominicans uptown. In the 1970s, after kingpin Nicky Barnes got locked up, drug trafficking in Harlem became decentralized. New York's Hispanic population had simultaneously mushroomed and, by the late 1980s, the Cubans and Dominicans had taken over the cocaine trade from Central and Upper Harlem through Washington Heights. "From 125th to 175th Street, there were enough places selling coke to sink the Queen Mary," George said. "For every one spot that closed, two more would open by the next day." In fact, many police officers were patrons themselves. For a time, George worked the doors of one after-hours spot called the Romper Room, on Amsterdam Avenue and 150th Street. His job was to collect guns at the door, but exceptions were made for the cops.

There were also the "legit" businesses where you could score. Many were on Saint Nicholas Avenue, just around the corner from our house: the Mark 4 and the Pink Angel (which were bars), the fish-and-chips spot, and the Chinese restaurant next door. These spots were dominated by young blacks from the neighborhood.

I maintained a comfortable distance apart at Manhattanville College—a small Catholic school in Purchase, New York, run by former nuns of the Sacred Heart. I had lazily picked the school because it was the alma mater of Mrs. Motley, my eleventh-grade English teacher, and I was too scared to go out to California, where I had always dreamed of going. In many ways, Manhattanville was ideal. I was a big fish in a small pond. By senior year, I had become a student adviser and was driving the college president around in a little Toyota Tercel—a status meted out to a few select students.

Coming from the city, Manhattanville seemed like a country club; all you had to do was prepare for class and take some tests and everything else was handed over on a silver plate. From Thursdays through Sundays, partying was a full-time gig. The drinking age was eighteen and, from the moment we set foot on campus for orientation, we were assailed with open kegs and sixteen-ounce cups, which the college used to bring students together.

There was a clear divide between black middle-class kids like me, who had experience in predominantly white environments, and black working-class and Higher Education Opportunity Program kids. The Black Student Union was largely made up of the latter. I had gone to a few of their events, but they never seemed to do much more than throw fashion shows.

Many black students saw me as the black guy who hung out with whites. I discovered this while conducting research for my senior thesis, which explored how differences in class shaped the experiences of black students at a predominantly white college. Many of them told me that they were surprised by my interest in the topic; they didn't think I liked black people. The fact that I didn't sit at the "black table" in the cafeteria or restrict my friendships to blacks raised suspicions about my race loyalties. At the same time, some of my white friends found it annoying that I was always harping on about race. Why couldn't I just get over it, like they had? After all, hadn't they accepted *me*?

My preoccupation with race didn't bring me any closer to finding community with other blacks. I found the African-American community very divided internally—by religious denomination, class, and even color prejudice—and I didn't fall neatly into any one group. I was a dark-skinned, middle-class black kid who had been raised in Harlem but educated and socialized outside, in upper-class Manhattan, with no real religious center and no black institution anchoring me. Church has always been the most powerful institution for blacks, but the Hayneses hadn't been to church since I was born. I hadn't even been baptized. I was too black for many whites and not black enough for many blacks. (Many years later, I would be characterized as an "Anglo dipped in chocolate" by a black therapist.) And so I became the black scholar who studies community while forever being in search of community.

When I first declared my major in sociology, I had no idea that my grandfather had been a sociologist himself. My father always referred to Pop Haynes as an "educator" and declined to say much more, unless it was to grumble about how shabbily the National Urban League later treated him. During my last year of college, I came across one of my grandfather's books in the library—*Negro Newcomers in Detroit*. Discouraged by its dense and dated prose, I quickly returned it to its shelf, but I had read enough to learn that he had been preoccupied with the very themes that were now consuming me—race, inequality, and segregation.

♥

It was a good time to be out of New York. The city was writhing from a national recession, and race relations hit an all-time low. Some white New Yorkers declared open season on black youths. In 1984, "Subway Vigilante" Bernhard Goetz became a folk hero to at least some New Yorkers when he shot four young black men after they allegedly tried to mug him on the Seventh Avenue express train. The Reverend Al Sharpton—then a sweatsuit-sporting Pentecostal preacher—rose to national prominence in the late 1980s, spearheading several "Days of Outrage," during which thousands of black protesters marched, halted subway service, and shut down the Brooklyn Bridge. In 1988, fifteen-year-old Tawana Brawley provoked the city's outrage again with her tale of being abducted, gang-raped, and smeared with feces by several white men—at least until it became apparent that she had concocted the whole story. For months, Sharpton and Brawley's two lawyers insisted that the city, as well as the state governor himself, was engaged in a racist cover-up. Spike Lee later captured the decade with his 1989 classic *Do the Right Thing*.

The explosion of crack cocaine ravaged black and Latino communities and led to unprecedented levels of violence and crime. A whole new arsenal of weapons—Uzis, MAC-10s, and Glocks—hit the streets, and turf wars between rival street dealers led to drive-by shootings and other gang-related murders. In 1982, Ronald Reagan launched the "War on Drugs" (although Nixon had initiated the war a decade earlier, declaring drug abuse "public enemy number one" and calling for a "new, all-out offensive" against it) and, in 1986, the Anti–Drug Abuse Act was passed. Although the law imposed mandatory minimum sentences for cocaine distribution, much harsher penalties were reserved for the distribution of crack cocaine, which was associated with blacks, than for powder cocaine. Just five grams of crack could earn a sentence of five to forty years; it took ten times that amount in powdered cocaine to earn an equivalent sentence. And while 86 percent of the law's $1.7 billion in funding went to prisons, interdictions, and law enforcement, only 14 percent was used for drug treatment, education, and prevention. Incarceration rates for black males in their teens and twenties skyrocketed over the next few decades.

Although crack received obsessive media attention, there was nothing new about burning cocaine. Older and more affluent users had discovered the intense rush of freebase—coke transformed into a rock you could smoke—beginning in the late 1970s. Freebase, derived by adding ether to extract impurities during the production process, was much more expensive than powdered cocaine, which had been "stepped on," or cut, at every stage of distribution. A gram of powdered cocaine became a half gram of freebase, and because users could smoke much more coke than they could ever shove up their nostrils, it became a vice that few could afford to maintain over time. That only added to its allure. In January 1979, the first cocaine extraction kit, which provided chemicals, glassware, and instructions for creating freebase, was introduced during New York's fashion week. By the early eighties, freebasing had become the rage among the elite of the music, film, and sports industries as well as among high rollers in the underground economy.

Freebasing was the right vice for its time. The early 1980s had seen the rise and rush of greed. Greed was glorified. This was the era of financial deregulation, hostile takeovers, decamillionaires, and brazen power brokers like Donald Trump, whom rappers idolized—right along with Scarface and Al Capone. Bling became the thing, and urban youth demonstrated status through heavy gold chains and leather jackets. It took money to freebase, and drug dealers were some of the heaviest users; it wasn't uncommon for a hustler to make $2,000 one day and be broke the next. Unlike powder cocaine, freebasing was not something you did to see you through the night; it was an event. It led to binge sessions of sex and coke that lasted for days on end. It shifted the drug scene out of the clubs and into the "base houses"—full-service operations where one could buy coke, smoke it, and sleep it off.

George was introduced to freebasing through a con woman he met at a Harlem bar. The con game was a man's world, and Candy—George's new acquaintance—needed a man to front for her. "If two women wanted to go off on their own," George explained, "they were shunned by the community." Although some of the more simple cons, like the bait and switch, could be pulled off alone, the big takings lay in more sophisticated maneuvers that required male cooperation. That's where George proved useful. He had the right look and enough swagger to convince Candy's male associates that she was working for him. One night, Candy turned him on to freebasing. More than thirty years later, he could still wax poetic on that first rush:

> Like standing on a beach and a forty-five-mile wind comes off the ocean on a cold day in November and slaps you in the face. Rain and everything. Problem is, after you get the first slap in the face you want to get a second, but you can't. You have to start at zero again.

After that first night, George would never return to snorting, which delivered a "measly tingle." Of course, there were times when he'd have to settle for smoking crack.

Unlike freebase, which shrank cocaine to its core, crack inflated it to five or six times its size. It was sold in small precooked units for a fraction of the cost of powder cocaine—a small glass vial went for as little as five bucks—ensuring a loyal customer base. By 1979, George had moved out of our parents' house and was rooming with Louis, a fellow user he had met through the Nation years back. Louis ran a Steak-N-Take, on 155th Street and Eighth Avenue, called the Mobile Kitchen (the kitchen was built into a bus) Louis and George became business partners. They sold reefer together in after-hours spots, and George helped him to manage the restaurant. The arrangement lasted about two years, until they were evicted for not paying rent. (Although my parents had been giving George rent money each month, he smoked it up.) Once again, George had to move back home, although he wasn't so welcome this time.

♥

George preferred coke dens to the after-hours spots because you could freebase openly. One spot that he fancied was Miss Anne's, on 150th Street and Saint Nicholas Avenue. Miss Anne was about sixty and was showing signs of decay from months, if not years, of freebasing. She didn't bathe and had a very strong stench to her. But you had to be in the know just to get into Miss Anne's. It was high end and drew the big players, some of whom threw extravagant coke parties at her house. George remembered one party, thrown by a Dominican dealer, where every patron received a gram of coke at the door, neatly wrapped in foil.

George met all sorts of people at Miss Anne's—neighborhood folks, stickup kids, crack dealers, pimps, and people just needing a place to fly and crash. He met two guys he had known from the Nation, who owned a building on Amsterdam Avenue; after getting deep into coke, they had turned it into a crack house.

One night, George met an air conditioner repairman—whom everyone called Dr. Fix It—lying in Miss Anne's bed. They got to talking and, over time, became buddies. George, feeling hemmed in back at our parents' house, thought Dr. Fix It would make a good roommate, and he proposed that they get a place together. Within weeks of moving in together, Dr. Fix It began inviting freebasers to hang out at their apartment. Eventually it became a coke den, which was not a bad thing from George's vantage, since it was customary for patrons to "pay the house"— that is, give the owner a token taste as a sign of goodwill. And some of the biggest patrons were coke dealers who had access to the best coke. You never knew what you'd come by at George's den—a dime bag or even a stolen brick (a kilo).

George and Fix It's den was not quite on a par with Miss Anne's. Although they aimed to draw the high-end users, they allowed crack now and again. "When you ran out of coke, you smoked crack." George was careful, though, to distinguish his operation from a crack house. "We weren't dealing and we weren't shooting. You could do anything at a crack house. We drew a line."

If crack was a big divider in the cocaine world, shooting was a bigger one. Hustlers didn't shoot. It was part of the cultural sense of who they were, and George saw himself as a hustler. They were a better class of people. In truth, many spots did double duty, although those that catered specifically to crack users were more dangerous, their clientele more desperate than strung out. Still, there was wide variation even from one crack house to the next. Some were full-service operations—both selling and providing a cozy space to get high. Others rented out the space for a small fee. George recalled one full-service crack house, near 116th Street, that required patrons to use the house pipe, thus ensuring that the crack residue could be reused. By this time, crack had become more than just a substitute for the "real thing."

George's memories of the next six or seven years become spotty here, but I remember them well. We had both moved back home—I from college, he from another eviction—and were sharing the first-floor room. He stayed up all night, writing cryptic, cosmic notes that I'd later find hidden in books—messages to and from God, laced with references to Allah and Yahweh and Jesus. He started calling himself Gabriel and creating his own cosmology. Some of the things George said were brilliant; others reminded me of the messages on Dr. Bronner's Magic Soaps—"Teaching the whole Human race our Eternal Father's great ALL-ONE-GOD-FAITH, as did the African astronomer Israel since the Year One"—or the pamphlets passed out by the Purple People of Central Park—"No leather shoes, read it while you're stoned." He was consumed with Egyptology and pyramidology, a pseudoscience focused on the Great Pyramid that emerged during the late nineteenth century and was later embraced by Jehovah's Witnesses, disciples of Carl Jung, and Afrocentrics alike. He made assertions that were at best questionable and sometimes verged on delusional. At one point, George claimed to be working undercover for the CIA. (Ironically, a conspiracy theory about the CIA pushing crack was circulating in the black community during this same time, which meant that George, who was becoming a crack addict, would be both a victim of and an accessory to the conspiracy.) He made conspicuously "covert" phone calls from our new digital phone, entering his secret code—which he took pains to let us see—and then covering his mouth, but not so much that we couldn't hear the weighty tone of the conversation. Silly though it sounds, he actually had us fooled for a while. He even had an impressive ID card, which, I later realized, he made in his Nefertiti Studio.

Once, as I was driving him through Harlem, he alerted me to a military truck just up ahead, which he claimed had been following us. "Oh, really?" I said. "But we're the ones behind the truck." Without batting an eye, he replied, "Oh, yeah, Brucie, they're assigned to provide me protection. I'm undercover!" The stories of my undercover brother suddenly seemed full of holes. When my parents and I confronted him, he unraveled. The more he talked, the less sense he made. It was as if we had broken a magic spell and sent him crashing down to earth. Although both my parents were social workers, and my mother had made a career in mental health care, they were only now beginning to recognize that their son was ill.

George was finally hospitalized. The doctors stabilized him with Haldol, an antipsychotic medication used to treat schizophrenia and bipolar disorder, and then transitioned him to lithium. I visited George regularly, always bringing cigarettes— Benson & Hedges 100s—and Swedish Fish gum candy. On one of my visits, a few weeks into his stay, I learned that the hospital planned to release him the next day. No outpatient plan had been put into place and no one had spoken with the family to discuss where he would live. My parents could no longer handle George at home, but they also couldn't handle his being released to the streets. We battled with his doctors to delay his discharge until we could make arrangements, and Pop used his neighborhood connections to swiftly set George up in an apartment— "a tiny cubbyhole called a room," as George later described it— on Saint Nicholas Terrace, a short walk from our home on Convent Avenue. Pop also paid for private psychiatric care, spending down his retirement savings to cover the tens of thousands of dollars in doctor fees that accrued over the next three years. It didn't help; George took any signs of improvement as proof that he wasn't ill and, invariably, stopped taking his medication.

By now, my parents' world had become so chaotic that they could barely keep track of their own affairs. The house was approaching its final stages of dysfunction. Pop had shut off the cold-water valve on the second floor to stop the pipes from leaking. Showers were out, of course, and the faulty plumbing in the bathroom obstructed the flow of hot water to the tub. Sponge baths, followed by a dash of Opium by Yves Saint Laurent, kept my mother fresh and fragrant.

The hole in the kitchen that surfaced in the 1960s was no longer the singular eyesore. The rest of the house had now caught up. Yellowing newspapers from the previous decade, and other rubbish, competed for floor space, creating an obstacle course through the front hallway, up the stairs, across the living room, and into the kitchen. Chairs were heaped with junk mail and empty water jugs, making "family time" impractical and unappealing.

Markers of opulence and squalor vied for attention. A red Oriental carpet, stretching twenty feet to the staircase, was fraying into nonexistence. A turn-of-the-century mahogany bookcase was blocked by a rolled-up carpet—deposited ten years earlier, on its return from the drycleaner—and virtually sealed shut from years of grime and disuse. Six beveled glass doors, each with a tiny lock and skeletal key, were flanked by fluted Corinthian columns, cresting at a bell-shaped capital with intricately carved scrolls and curly acanthus leaves. But such ornamental details were lost on the observer. Layers of dust had concealed the sheen of the mahogany and the delicate architectural motifs that were mirrored throughout the house. The bookcase had been custom built and still held my grandparents' treasured books: the collected poems of Burns, Longfellow, Tennyson, and Dunbar; the essays of Emerson, Weber, Spencer, and Mills; a 1937 edition of *Up from Slavery*, signed by the son of Booker T. Washington; and, of course, the works that my grandparents had authored themselves—*Unsung Heroes*, *The Black Boy of Atlanta*, and *The Trend of the Races*.

♦

At points, George resembled the crazy people I used to see on Broadway, mumbling to themselves or cursing at anything and everything walking by. When he got money, he spent it on crack. When the drugs wore off, he was back on the streets, self-medicating. Each psychotic episode was more punishing than the last. He became threatening if he didn't get what he wanted, which was usually money. Once, when he was visiting our parents, he pushed our mother. Pop threw him out of the house, and George threw a bottle through the living room window in retaliation.

I was now living in Yonkers but was called home for each new crisis. Sometimes we were forced to call Harlem Hospital's Crisis Intervention Unit and the police at the same time. We had a whole routine: I'd drive down from Yonkers and Pop, in his seventies now, would race the seven blocks up Convent Avenue and across to Saint Nicholas Place to get to George before the cops did. We were afraid they'd kill him. Sometimes we'd find George running through the streets and have to chase him down. We also needed to make sure he got to a hospital, which is what the intervention team was good for. Over the years, George would spend time cycling in and out of Harlem Hospital, Mount Sinai, Columbia Presbyterian Hospital, and Lincoln Hospital. His diagnosis would change with each facility. And because there was never any coordination between the discharge unit and social services, he'd often be released before a structured outpatient plan was put in place.

Reforms to the mental health system in the 1960s and early 1970s had deinstitutionalized a vast number of mentally ill and disabled. Rampant abuse at state-run institutions, like Willowbrook, had been exposed in the early 1970s, and advances in psychiatric drugs encouraged the treatment of patients through outpatient care. By the 1980s, the city was releasing the mentally ill after a single day of treatment, a fact that helped fuel the rising homelessness crisis.

At the age of thirty-four, George was finally diagnosed with bipolar disorder. His symptoms were textbook: he couldn't sleep for days, became consumed with ideas he believed were brilliant (sometimes they were, sometimes they spun into psychosis), then he'd crash into a deep depression. He was put on antipsychotic drugs but never stayed on them for long; instead, he self-medicated with cocaine and alcohol, drifting back and forth from psychiatric hospitals and drug rehabilitation clinics to the streets of Harlem. Ironically, my mother was now working at the Washington Heights Community Mental Health Center, on 145th Street and Amsterdam Avenue, treating a whole generation of black men who, like George, were dually diagnosed as mentally ill and chemically addicted—referred to back then as MICA patients.

The psychiatry ward at Harlem Hospital was probably the scariest facility, not only for the patients but also for their visitors. There may have been some traffic during the week, but on weekends the place was deserted—no reception desk, no security guard—and that's when I usually went. Walking into the lobby was like entering a deserted subway station—a little too quiet, with lots of passageways for hiding and no one to hear you scream. The one elevator was controlled by the ward and was released on a case-by-case basis; I had to get on the phone—often waiting ten or more minutes for someone to pick up—and ask to have it sent back down. The ward itself was a caricature of a mental hospital, its occupants all in different states of catatonia. People didn't walk so much as shuffle. The staff didn't engage with patients, except to administer medication. How could they be getting counseling if they couldn't even zip up their flies? The few doctors I ever saw there were foreign-born and seemed to know as much about Harlem as the average Harlemite knew about Karachi.

♥

My grandfather's second wife, Olyve Love Jeter Haynes (whom my father, and consequently the rest of us, still stubbornly referred to as Miss Jeter), died in the early 1980s. We were contacted by her son (whose existence shocked us all) and invited to come out to Mount Vernon to collect Pop Haynes's belongings. Many years earlier, I had accompanied my father to the Mount Vernon house, at 303 Tecumseh Avenue—a stately white colonial on a corner lot—on one of his rare trips to visit his father's widow. I was about seven years old and marveled at how elegant the house was. Everything had seemed dainty and pristine: the petite upholstered chairs, the delicate antique tables positioned squarely in front of each chair, and the crystal candy dishes—filled with starlight mints, peppermint ribbons, and horehound drops— that embellished every table. All of the dishes had tops to protect the candy, and it was understood that reaching inside uninvited was an act of impertinence. I learned to sit patiently and stare at the dish until Miss Jeter noticed and offered me a candy.

Now, as a man in my twenties, I returned to the house alone. I was struck immediately by how stuffy and pretentious it all was; the countless knickknacks that I had once taken for high culture now struck me as a little ridiculous. Miss Jeter's son was a kindly, light-skinned man in his sixties who, I learned, was a trained classical musician like his mother. He took me upstairs to my grandfather's study. The room had a shrine-like quality, as if Miss Jeter hadn't moved a thing since Pop Haynes's passing twenty-five years earlier. All of his manuscripts were organized and his letters were stacked and bound with twine. The colossal oak desk, which he had inherited from his days at Yale University, dominated the small study, and one could imagine my grandfather entering the room at any moment to resume an important project, except that all of the writing utensils seemed to have vanished.

That afternoon, I brought home a dozen or so boxes filled with books, manuscripts, newspaper clippings, letters, and historical mementoes, and deposited the bulk of them in the second-floor hallway. They remained there for another ten years, which was just enough time for the leaking roof to obliterate a good part of Pop Haynes's history. (Years later, when I began working on this book and was scouring the archives at Yale and Columbia universities, in vain, for a copy of my grandfather's memoir, I realized that we had probably had it all along.)

Fortunately, I had taken a few of the more promising-looking boxes back to my apartment in Yonkers, although I didn't explore them until years later. My own life was pressing ahead. With a college degree in hand and elite prep school credentials behind me, I was ready to earn my fair share of the new corporate wealth that had landed in New York. I had taken several courses in business administration during my last year of college to prepare for an entry-level job in marketing or sales. But most corporations steered me to the personnel or human resources departments, where none of the power and most of the blacks were kept. With few options, I started driving school buses— first for Champions Sports Club and later for SuperTrans—and coaching peewee soccer. Even these jobs, which catered to the children of elite New York private schools like Dalton, Fieldston, Horace Mann, and Riverdale Country School, were landed through my connections at the prep school I attended before college.

For a while, it looked like this would be my life, but serendipity intervened. I regularly played pickup soccer in Central Park's Sheep Meadow, where a handful of women occasionally joined in. One of them, a graduate student at Columbia University, took a sisterly interest in me and, after learning that I had majored in sociology, offered to introduce me to the brilliant and eccentric sociologist Jay Schulman.

Jay was the founder of the National Jury Project and was one of the first to apply the social sciences to the selection of juries— determining through surveys and focus groups the characteristics that most strongly predicted how a potential juror would vote. This information would then inform the voir dire—the questioning of prospective jurors—and the exercise of peremptory challenges, to shape the most favorable jury for the defense. His techniques helped spawn a multimillion-dollar trial consulting industry as well as a generation of psychological research on juries.

A staunch opponent of the Vietnam War, Jay had worked on behalf of the era's most infamous activists, including Benjamin Spock, the Chicago Seven, and the Harrisburg Seven. Dr. Spock, the pediatrician and author of the 1946 bestseller *The Common Sense Book of Baby and Child Care*, had become a political agitator by the 1960s, campaigning for nuclear disarmament and protesting the war in Vietnam. "There's no point in raising children if they're going to be burned alive," he famously said. In 1968, he was tried—and later convicted—for advocating the destruction of draft cards. The defense team appealed, claiming that the jury had been stacked. Of the one hundred potential jurors in the original—and purportedly randomly selected—pool, only nine had been women. Public opinion polls had shown that women were much more sympathetic to the antiwar movement than men were and thus were more likely to find the defendant not guilty. The defense team analyzed the jury pools that had been drawn for the seven judges in the district during the prior two and a half years and found that one judge, in particular, had consistently fewer women in his juror pools. Of course, it was the judge presiding over the Spock case. The defense successfully appealed the decision, and Dr. Spock was eventually exonerated—though on the basis of the First Amendment.

One of Jay's most publicized cases was that of the so-called Harrisburg Seven, in which a group of Catholic antiwar activists—most of them nuns and priests—were indicted by the federal government on charges of conspiracy to raid federal offices, bomb government buildings, and kidnap Henry Kissinger, who was then the national security advisor to Richard Nixon. Jay was approached by the defense team, which was headed by Ramsey Clark, the former United States attorney general, to help select the jury. Using data collected from nearly one thousand community-based surveys, Jay showed that the initial jury pool drawn for the case was not representative of the Harrisburg community and that it would likely favor the prosecution team. After convincing the judge to call for a new pooling of potential jurors, he designed a more comprehensive survey to assess community sentiments about the case, attitudes about the war, and trust in the government. He constructed a profile of the ideal juror for the defense: a female Democrat with a white-collar or skilled blue-collar occupation and no particular religious preference. After a week of deliberations, and a hung jury, the charges were dismissed.

By the time I met Jay, he had broken with the National Jury Project, having grown too radical for the group, and perhaps too eccentric. Over six feet tall, with an imposing belly, a long, unkempt beard, and a massive head with shaggy white hair, Jay looked like Zeus on a bad day. He was manic-depressive, half blind in one eye, and smoked incessantly. He yelled and banged on tables. He cursed like a sailor. It could be embarrassing being out with him in public. At the same time, he taught me how to command power in society. He could literally make a bank open its doors after hours and let him walk out with a wad of money!

I had brought my résumé to my job interview, but he never even gave it a glance. He looked me over, asked a few pointed questions, and sized me up. This was, after all, what he did for a living. Over the next four years, I worked with him on some of the highest-profile cases of the decade—the Weather Underground (1984), *Westmoreland v. CBS* (1984), and Howard Beach (1987)—not to mention the many insider trading cases emblematic of the decade of greed.

My first case was probably the biggest. From a house in Larchmont, in Westchester County, I conducted a network analysis of the jury pool for the Weather Underground Brink's robbery case. The analysis drew heavily on the work of social psychologist Stanley Milgram, whose 1967 small-world experiment revealed that there were just five or six links—or degrees of separation— between any two individuals. Beginning only with Jay's personal Rolodex, contacts of the defense attorney, and the jury pool list, I made cold calls to find someone who knew a prospective juror. I was shocked by how much detailed information I could get about a total stranger through extended social networks and a properly phrased query. "Hi, John, you don't know me, but so and so said that you might be able to help me. I am wondering if you happen to know X or someone who lives in X's town or on X's street." About 90 percent of the time, I was able to zero in on a juror within five or six calls.

About two years after I started working for Jay, he told me that I couldn't work for him forever and that no one was going to listen to me if I didn't have a PhD. To support me through school, he agreed to strike a deal: he'd continue to pay my full salary if I promised to read everything—every book and article assigned by my professors—three times. I kept my end of the bargain for at least a year.

I had long wondered why this radical Jewish lefty would defend General William Westmoreland, who had led the U.S. forces in Vietnam between 1964 and 1968. I finally summoned the nerve to ask him. He said that everyone deserved a fair trial, and those who could afford to pay—and they paid dearly if they hired him—helped subsidize those who couldn't. That's what later allowed us to do pro bono work for Charles Hynes, the state special prosecutor on the Howard Beach case. Howard Beach was a quiet suburban community in Queens, New York, that made national news in 1986 after a mob of white youths, armed with baseball bats, attacked three black men who had stumbled into their neighborhood. One of the victims, Michael Griffith, was chased onto the Belt Parkway and hit by a car.

In his firsthand account of the Howard Beach trial, Hynes recalls his initial uneasiness with Schulman's politics and methods:

> Like a garage mechanic taking a motor apart, he broke down prospective jurors by demographic components—age, race, sex, neighborhood, career salary—each of which was an element that might affect the vote . . . I still preferred to choose my jury based on the question-and-answer philosophy, laced with a heavy dose of gut instinct.

Three of the defendants in the case ultimately were convicted of manslaughter, but Jay never lived to see it. At age sixty-eight, he suffered a massive heart attack and died before the trial concluded. I never got the chance to thank him for what he did for me.

For years, I've tried to make sense of my fate and that of my brothers. There's so much that amounted to timing. I became a professor because I got a PhD, because I met Jay Schulman, because I met a graduate student who knew Jay Schulman, because I played soccer in Central Park, because I went to prep school where I learned to play soccer. I'm not the best or the brightest and was never even particularly ambitious. I figured I'd get a secure job at a community college when I graduated, a reasonable goal for an average kid like me. George was the brilliant one but, ten years my senior, he got caught up in the maelstrom of the sixties. Alan was killed because he was working at a small bike shop on a sweltering day in August and its narrow width couldn't hold more than a few customers at a time. A long line of customers formed outside the door in the midday sun, and two men got tired of waiting and raised a ruckus. It was Alan's face they saw, and it was Alan's face they waited for later.

9

KEEP ON KEEPIN' ON

AVID Dinkins, the first—and, as of this writing, the only—African-American mayor of New York City, was sworn into office in 1989, just as the city's ethnic groups were colliding on the national stage. Blacks boycotted Korean groceries in Brooklyn, and Leonard Jeffries, professor of Black Studies at the City University of New York, rose to prominence for his controversial claims that Jews had financed the slave trade. In August 1991, a riot broke out in Crown Heights, Brooklyn. West Indians attacked Jews from the local Hasidic community in retaliation for the accidental killing of Gavin Cato, the seven-year-old son of Guyanese immigrants. The three-day riot, which many Jews characterized as a pogrom, ended in the slaying of the Australian student Yankel Rosenbaum.

Despite the racial tensions, crime actually dropped during Dinkins's one term (although his administration would be disparaged as ineffective). Harlem, too, became safer and more livable: new water mains were laid, sewers were dug, sidewalks were paved, and the streets were better lit. The Upper Manhattan Empowerment Zone brought $300 million in new development funds and almost as much in tax breaks to businesses investing in Harlem, although little went to local black businesses.

Middle- and upper-middle-class black professionals began moving back to Harlem, where sprawling brownstones could still be had for a song. Many of them, like our own, were in poor condition.

The house had reached its final stages of ruin. The roof was now beyond repair, and my father, who had been patching it up for years, was too old to even pretend to be tinkering. Hundreds of bottles of Poland Spring water, all in different stages of use and age, had amassed on the ground floor. My parents' worlds had become unmanageable.

A dim fluorescent light silhouetted the balustrade on the way up to the second floor. Vying for space on the landing were a wire shopping cart, twenty-five-pound bags of salt, and fifty-pound tubs of tar. (Well into his seventies, Pop had carried these tubs up three flights of stairs to the fire escape alcove, where a fireman's ladder led to the leaking roof. Once on the roof, he used a makeshift pulley system—a rope looped around the top of the ladder—to pull up the massive tar tubs.) On either end of the second-floor hallway, two identical doors faced each other. One never opened; it had been bolted from the inside for at least thirty years. The other, locked with a single dead bolt whenever we went out, was the bedroom my parents once shared. Now my father slept there alone. Overgrown snake plants and coleus poked through broken wooden blinds. My father was apparently still watering them. Heavy gold curtains shut out the world.

A delicate satin sofa, its center leg broken, its frame split in the center, had become a resting place for decades-old tax files and receipt books. A rickety typewriter table with a vintage desktop Remington was wedged behind it. To the right was a Castro convertible bed. The sheets, stained and discolored, had taken on the rancid smell of the old man who occupied them. Stacks of old newspapers—the *New York Times*, the *Amsterdam News*, the *Daily News*, the *New York Post*, and sometimes the

Wall Street Journal—were stockpiled across the floor, making walking precarious.

Much the same could be said for the rest of the house, as my parents tried to keep up with an aging building and their aging bodies—as the pipes broke and the electrical wiring became outdated, as the paint peeled, as the roof failed and the ceiling leaked, as the rugs became threadbare and the dust settled.

Pop was dying. Cancer and heart disease had taken their toll, and it was George, now in his forties, who stepped in to feed him, clothe him, change him, and keep him company. By now, George was making progress in a residential drug treatment program and had advanced from a halfway to a three-quarter recovery house, where he was granted unsupervised leave time to take care of Pop. For the first time in decades, father and son actually listened to each other. George told him of his break with the Nation and his embrace of more moderate Islam. Pop revealed that, for months, he had been meeting with a rabbi downtown, and he showed George the yarmulke that he kept tucked away. He never explained why he was drawn to Judaism, and perhaps George never asked. Our family wasn't hardwired for psychological probing.

My mother's attention had long since shifted to me. With Alan's death and George's illness, I had become the repository for all her hopes and dreams. And when I started showing signs that I just might deliver, her tentacles grew strong. In my last year at the City University of New York Graduate Center, I landed an interview with Yale University for an assistant professorship appointment. I shared the news with my parents but, because I considered Yale out of my league, I made it clear to them that I didn't want the news broadcast. But that is exactly what my mother did. The Saturday before my interview, I met her at Saks and, as we passed by the cosmetics counters, a saleswoman called out, "Is this the one who's going to Yale?" I was furious.

We had been there to buy clothes for me—a "few things," as my mother had put it, "for the big day." I took this to mean a sweater or maybe a nice shirt, but she had an entire new wardrobe in mind—a European three-piece suit, Italian wingtip shoes, and a full-length cashmere coat. This last item we argued about. I already had a perfectly fine blazer; it was five or six years old but still in good shape. Yet she was convinced that I needed to dress for Yale like I belonged there.

The morning after my interview, she called to tell me about her dream from the previous night. In it, I was giving my job talk when suddenly all the Yale professors rose at once and gave me a standing ovation. She asked me if this had actually happened. As absurd as the question was, I was sorry to disappoint her.

My mom saw my dissertation defense as my coming-out party. She wanted not only to attend but also to bring her friends. I had heard stories about parents showing up at their kids' defense but, as I later learned, this meant that they waited in the bar area on the eighteenth floor. My request must have seemed very bizarre to my committee but, stranger still, they agreed to let her attend. My mom arrived in her finest clothes and jewelry, surrounded by her entourage. When, in the middle of my defense, my adviser, Stephen Steinberg, made a historical reference to Russian Jews, my mother's best friend, Blossom, an assertive Jewish woman with strong opinions of her own, took offense and began arguing with him. To add to this, my mom looked miffed every time I was challenged on some point in my research. She seemed not to understand that the main point of a dissertation defense was to defend your dissertation. As we wound down, Steinberg turned to my mother and, with great respect, asked if there was anything she might like to say about the proceedings. She beamed and said that, although the committee had been very tough on me, I had handled myself very well.

When I finally got my PhD, I wrote a letter to my parents. It was uncharacteristically gushy. I told them how I much I loved them, which was something we never said in our family. I thanked them for the countless sacrifices they had made; I needed to let them know how important they'd been to my success. True to form, my mother made multiple copies of the letter and handed them out to all her friends and coworkers, the ladies at Saks, and, of course, her manicurist, Tina.

Although I often complained that my mother was overly involved in my life, I see now that I was a party to it. When I first met Syma—the woman who would become my wife—I found myself wanting my mother's approbation. Like my brother Alan's wife, Marcia, Syma was Jewish. I knew that race and religion didn't matter to my mother, but still I wondered if she'd see in Syma what I saw. And so, after our first date, when I told Syma that I wanted her to come down to Saks the next Saturday to meet my mother, she looked at me like I was crazy. Nevertheless, she agreed to go.

We met my mom at the Saks nail salon and had lunch at Café SFA, on the eighth floor. She liked Syma immediately and was impressed with her Ivy League education, her background in classical music, and the fact that she was teaching public school kids in Harlem. Syma was the first woman my mom saw as being able to hold her own at the sophisticated faculty cocktail parties she envisioned me attending one day. She also liked the way that Syma lit up when I talked, how she seemed to find me as smart as my mom did.

When Syma and I got back to my apartment, later that day, there was a message waiting for me on my machine. Syma stood in shock as she listened to my mom reporting with glee that she had just gotten off the phone with a friend who happened to work at Syma's school (my mom's network was extensive) and that Syma had received a good review. After that, Syma could do no wrong.

Within a few months, Mom started dropping hints to me about getting married. "Don't let this one go," she said. And I didn't. Syma and I married in the summer of 1995, just days before I was to leave for my new job at Yale. Pop died that next December.

I had pleaded with my father for years to recount the family's history before it was lost forever. Not long after he passed away, I found a cassette he had made on the occasion of my thirty-fifth birthday, just days before our last Thanksgiving together. Much of the recording is devoted to his early childhood—memories of train rides through the South ("with gaslights and, of course, in a Jim Crow car"), of the Apperson Jack Rabbit car that the family later bought, of a sandwich of sardines and Uneeda biscuits that his father made on one of their journeys. These weren't the memories I'd been hoping for. There were no juicy morsels about Du Bois or even about his own father. He offered no original insights on growing up in the black bourgeoisie or on coming of age during the Harlem Renaissance.

Instead, Pop described the buckboard, which he called a "bug boy" ("similar to a buggy but with no back to it"), that awaited the family at the train station in Letohatchee, Alabama, and the three-mile journey to Big Mama's farm. His parents rode in the seat upfront while he bounced around in the back, feeling every rock and pebble along the long, dusty road. He recalled the little store they stopped at along the way: "Cookies were not sold in small boxes back then but in huge boxes, two foot square. The proprietor would reach in, scoop up the cookies or crackers or whatever you wanted, and weigh them—on a large scale, of course." I found it both touching and maddening that a man at the end of his life would bring such care and loving detail to bear upon a box of cookies. These cherished memories of eight decades past were his parting gift to me.

Perhaps the greatest treasure on the cassette was the memory of a letter that his father once wrote to him: "I have my first letter from your grandfather, that is, my father. It starts out, 'My dear little boy,' and so on. It's here . . . somewhere in the house. Maybe it'll turn up."

It did turn up, years later, when I was clearing out the house. Dated July 16, 1916, it was written just one day before my father's fourth birthday:

> *My dear little Boy,*
> *Father would like so very much to be with you tomorrow on*
> *your fourth birthday. Four years old you are. Father thinks you*
> *have been a good boy to take care of mother while he is away,*
> *and he is going to bring you something good when he comes. I*
> *hope you have learned the names of some of the birds you have*
> *seen in the woods, and that you have worked in the garden to*
> *help mother. You must put this letter away to keep and to read*
> *when your next birthdays come.*
> *Your loving father,*
>
> *George Edmund Haynes*

The little boy would heed these words and would treasure this token of his father's affection in the final days of his life. It seemed to be one of the few surviving mementos from his father that he had to cling to. Another was a photograph of the two of them, circa 1913, at Big Mama's farm: Edmund, a little tyke, sits propped up on his father's knee. He wears a white frock and stares wide-eyed at the camera. His father, dapper and distinguished in a dark, crisply pressed three-piece suit and a starched white shirt buttoned to the top, sits on a wooden armchair that seems a bit formal for the narrow country porch. He fashions just a hint of a smile. The melting snow suggests a late-winter day.

When he became a father himself, Ed doted on his sons, spending time that he had never had with his own father. He took us to museums. He played ball with us in the park. He told us bedtime stories and read to us—often from the Negro biographies that his own mother had authored and dedicated to him. He came to every one of my soccer games—often the only parent cheering from the sidelines. And yet, for all his efforts, he too was destined to disappoint as a father. My brother George used to chastise him for not standing up to our mother, for letting her push him around. George, who yearned for a strong patriarchal family, later found what he was looking for in the black nationalist politics of the 1960s.

And although my father personified the tough undercover detective who held his own in the roughest of neighborhoods, he was unable to keep my brother Alan safe in his own stomping grounds. Despite an eyewitness account and the inside connections my father had in law enforcement, he was powerless in moving the city to pursue Alan's murderer. With the soaring murder rate of young black men across New York City during the 1970s, black life was cheap, and Alan's death became another statistic that warranted no further investigation. Even in the face of such personal injustice, my father conducted himself beyond reproach to the very end.

Looking back, I can see that my father was a man one step out of time, in a world moving just a little bit too quickly. If he could only slow it down a notch, it would all be fine.

❤

With total control of the family finances after my father died, Daisy began sending lavish care packages to our home in

Connecticut. Every week, choice prime meats and fresh seafood were FedExed overnight from Citarella's, the gourmet food market on the Upper West Side. Jumbo shrimp, loin lamb chops, filet mignon, Cornish game hens, eight-inch-long grey sole fillets a quarter inch thick. She must have spent more than $200 a week on our groceries. But it cost us plenty, too: each night she'd call to find out what we'd eaten, and no matter how we responded, she was dissatisfied. If we praised the fish, she prodded, "Not the steak? You didn't want the steak?" If the steak, why not the chicken? If the chicken, why not the fish? As much as we loved these luxuries, which we never could have afforded on my assistant professor's salary, Syma pressed to put a stop to the packages and phone calls. They both ended abruptly, in fall 1997, when my mother was diagnosed with pancreatic cancer.

Right up to the end, she never lost her sense of glamour. A few days before she was to be admitted to Mount Sinai Hospital, we bought a sumptuous white fleece robe from Macy's for her hospital stay. The label was Stan Herman. My mom graciously accepted the gift and then, as we later found out, went to Saks and bought herself a Christian Dior robe. Even while undergoing daily rounds of toxic chemicals, she wanted to make a good appearance. The day before she began her chemotherapy, she was wheeled into Saks to get a manicure and pedicure. As she passed the counters she had patronized for years, she queen-waved to everyone. Nothing could strip her of her sense of pride.

She died an undignified death, though, on a hospital toilet, of a heart attack, only a few days into her chemo. Her friend Lavanna was with her at the end. She called and gave me second-to-second updates as the doctors pumped my mother's heart. For about fifteen minutes, I clutched the phone helplessly, praying, crying. And then Lavanna said the doctors hadn't been able to save her. She was gone. My first thought was, *No more phone calls for Brucie.* No one would ever need to hear my voice so much again.

Emptying the house was beyond me. Here in this heap of battered furniture and faded newspapers, one-of-a-kind tables coated with grease and grime, everything seemed precious and useless. When I reached the third floor, innocent times came flooding back. Despite the debris that jammed the hallways and master kitchen, two rooms remained largely untouched. These had been our playrooms, and the remnants from all three of our childhoods remained behind: Spalding High-Bounce Balls that had long lost their bounce, boxes of Lionel trains and train tracks, antique metal trucks with busted wheels, building blocks and slot car sets, a wooden Pinocchio doll that stretched at the limbs, a water-damaged antique desk, unused pieces from model car kits, Monopoly money and board game pieces. Retrieving a faded View-Master, I flipped through images of Robin Hood and his merry men.

After taking what I hoped were the most valuable contents, I hired a crew and solicited help from neighbors to remove the rest—beat-up furniture, stacks of books too old to salvage, mounds of papers too scattered to piece through. Dumpsters were filled with the sweetness and anarchy that had been our lives, then hauled off to a landfill somewhere in the Bronx.

Despite the home's condition, it still contained the original woodwork and marble tiles. Few Harlemites could afford to purchase and patch up such an enormous house—even at the bargain prices for Harlem real estate in the late 1990s—and long-time residents made clear their concerns about who would be their next neighbors. Numbers runners and nefarious characters were the only local folks who had the cash to buy it. One charlatan, reportedly a Wall Street broker, came by, children in tow, claiming to be seeking a family residence. It turned out he had already gobbled up three around the block. In the end, it was the video jockey and documentary filmmaker Fab 5 Freddy who bought the home, signaling the arrival of a new class of black folk to the Heights. Over the coming years, our block drew well-to-do whites, and blacks, in search of enormous estates within Manhattan. An enormous turreted mansion three blocks south of our house was the setting of Wes Anderson's 2001 film *The Royal Tenenbaums*.

In 1992, the Body Shop opened a branch on 125th Street; Ben & Jerry's, Starbucks, and Capezio soon followed. Sociologist Sharon Zukin would later describe this changing retail landscape as the "boutiquing" of Harlem. Luxury doorman buildings, where apartments go for a million dollars, pull in black and white middle-class New Yorkers and push out working-class residents. Though I am now a tenured professor and live in a thriving college town in Northern California, I could never afford to buy my way back into the Harlem I grew up in.

In 2001, my first book—*Red Lines, Black Spaces: The Politics of Race and Space in a Black Middle-Class Suburb*—was released. My wife and I threw a huge party to celebrate. Although we had recently moved to Davis, California, and were just beginning to build a new community, there must have been sixty people in our house. Syma surprised me with an enormous custom-made chocolate cake shaped as a book, with raspberry lines running through it (to represent the "red lines" of the book's title)—an extravagance my mother would have appreciated.

It was a tremendous moment of accomplishment. I had made it to a first-rate university, my first book had been published, and tenure finally seemed attainable. It should have been the happiest moment of my life. Yet, as I rose to say a few words of thanks to the group, all I could think of was my parents and brothers, and that nobody was there to see me now. I'd never felt lonelier.

When I grapple with that question made famous by David Byrne—"Well, how did I get here?"—I think of the phrases I've come to take for granted—"Keep on movin'!" . . . "Keep on keepin' on!"—and I realize that my parents protected me from much of the racism that characterizes black existence outside of Harlem and that I was fortunate to come across the "right kind" of white people in the environments my parents placed me in. And we, of course, appeared to be the "right kind" of black people. In fact, to those who never got past the double doors of my childhood home, we looked much like the model black family—cultured, dignified, and self-assured. This book is a tribute to that family, which was never as carefree as the image we fashioned for the world, never as secure in our futures, each generation walking a tightrope, one misstep from free fall.

NOTES

PREFACE

p. xv   *Portraits of Outstanding Americans of Negro Origin*: In 1943, the
Harmon Foundation commissioned the Harlem Renaissance artist Laura Wheeler Waring, along with Betsy Graves Reyneau, to
paint portraits for an exhibit entitled *Portraits of Outstanding Americans of Negro Origin*. Of the twenty-three portraits commissioned
for this series, eight were painted by Waring: W. E. B. Du Bois,
Marian Anderson, Harry T. Burleigh, Brigadier General Benjamin Oliver Davis, Lillian Evanti, James Weldon Johnson, Dr.
Leslie P. Hill, and George Edmund Haynes. The exhibit premiered
at the Smithsonian Institution in 1944 and then toured the country from 1944 to 1954. (During the national tour, some twenty-two
portraits were added to the original twenty-three.) In 1967, forty-
one of the cumulative fifty portraits were donated to the National
Portrait Gallery. In 1997, the National Portrait Gallery partially
reconstructed the historic show with the donated portraits. See
Tuliza K. Fleming, introduction to *Breaking Racial Barriers: African Americans in the Harmon Foundation Collection* (Pomegranate
Press, 1997).

p. xv   Generational occupational status and differences between blacks
and whites: Peter Blau and Otis Duncan, *The American Occupational Structure* (Free Press, 1967).

1. MAD MONEY

p. 1 Alexander Hamilton's estate was perched high on a hill and over-
looked the Hudson River to the west and the Harlem and East
Rivers to the east. The entire property—which Hamilton accumulated through three separate purchases between 1800 and
1803—ran from what is today 140th Street to 147th Street and was
bisected by Bloomingdale Road (later Old Broadway). The two-
story Federal home stood at 143rd Street and Convent Avenue.
There, Hamilton planted a row of thirteen sweet gum trees (one
for each state). All were uprooted in 1908. See Frank Bergen
Kelley, *Historical Guide to the City of New York* (Forgotten Books,
2015), 151, 404; Ron Chernow, *Alexander Hamilton* (Penguin
Books, 2005), 641–43; and New York City Landmarks Preservation Commission, *Hamilton Heights/Sugar Hill Historic District
Extension, Designation Report* (October 23, 2001), 4.

p. 1 On early grand estates of Harlem Heights, see Chernow, *Alexander Hamilton*; Harold C. Syrett, *The Papers of Alexander Hamilton*
(Columbia University Press, 1977), 25:38–39; Michael Henry
Adams, *Harlem: Lost and Found* (Monacelli Press, 2002), 117–21,
125–37; Andrew S. Dolkart and Gretchen S. Sorin, *Touring Historic Harlem: Four Walks in Northern Manhattan* (New York Landmarks Conservancy, 1997), 7–16, 94, 107; Kelley, *Historical Guide to
the City of New York*, 151, 404; New York City Landmarks Preservation Commission, *Hamilton Heights/Sugar Hill*.

p. 1 The Pinehurst mansion would remain with the family through the
1860s, when the era of the grand estates of Harlem Heights came
to an end. By the 1830s, the city's reservoirs were no longer adequate to serve the rapidly growing population, and outbreaks of
cholera and yellow fever ravaged the city. In 1837, the city began
construction of the Croton Aqueduct to bring fresh water from
upstate New York. The aqueduct cut right through the Bradhurst
estate by way of Tenth Avenue, elevating the land directly behind
the mansion and obstructing its views. By the 1860s, the Bradhurst family began subdividing the property and selling off lots.
Eventually, the Pinehurst mansion became the Mount Saint
Vincent Hotel. See Hudson River Museum of Westchester, *The Old
Croton Aqueduct: Rural Resources Meet Urban Needs* (Hudson River

Museum of Westchester, 1992), 14–18; New York City Landmarks Preservation Commission, *Hamilton Heights/Sugar Hill*, 4; John B. Jervis, "Description of the Croton Aqueduct," *Documents of the Senate of the State of New York* 4 (1842), 11–27; and Augustus Maunsell Bradhurst, *My Forefathers: Their History from Records & Traditions* (De La More Press, 1910), chapters 6 and 7.

p. 1   Improvements in urban mass transit led to mass speculation uptown: Gilbert Osofsky, *Harlem: The Making of a Ghetto* (Ivan R. Dee, 1996), 87–91.

p. 2   Live-in servants in Harlem Heights in the late 1800s: New York City Landmarks Preservation Commission, *Hamilton Heights/ Sugar Hill*, 14.

p. 5   The only store in New York City with its own slot car racetrack: Claire Berman, "Comparison-Shopping in Toyland," *New York* (December 7, 1970): 74.

p. 6   Horace Mann sex scandals: Jenny Anderson, "Retired Horace Mann Teacher Admits to Sex with Students," *New York Times* (June 23, 2012); and Marc Fisher, "The Master," *New Yorker* (April 1, 2013).

p. 8   References to Dr. Richard Dobson and Virginia Lumpkin in *Jet* magazine (October 27, 1960): 63.

p. 9   Numbers of adults playing bridge in 1958: Robert D. Putnam, *Bowling Alone: The Collapse and Revival of American Community* (Simon & Schuster, 2000), 103.

p. 9   Indictment of the black middle class for reproducing social conventions of whites: E. Franklin Frazier, *Black Bourgeoisie* (The Free Press, 1957), 204 (first published in France, two years earlier, as *Bourgeoisie Noire*).

p. 17   Rosetta LeNoir: Obituaries by Douglas Martin, *New York Times* (March 20, 2002); and Michael Carson, *Guardian* (March 26, 2002). Rosetta credited Orson Welles as being "the only one who had faith that blacks could bring the right dignity and sophistication to Shakespeare."

2. NOT ALMS BUT OPPORTUNITY

p. 27   Arkansas law barring free education for blacks: John Hope Franklin, *Reconstruction After the Civil War* (University of Chicago Press, 1961), 46.

p. 27 Bibliographical material on George Haynes: Daniel J. Perlman, *Stirring the White Conscience* (unpublished dissertation, New York University, 1972); Francill Rusan Wilson, *The Segregated Scholars: Black Social Scientists and the Creation of Black Labor Studies, 1890–1950* (University of Virginia Press, 2006); Samuel K. Roberts, "George Edmund Haynes: Advocate for Interracial Cooperation," in *Black Apostles: Afro-American Clergy Confront the Twentieth Century*, ed. Randall K. Burkett and Richard Newman (G. K. Hall, 1978), 97–127; and Ralph E. Luker, *The Social Gospel in Black and White: American Radical Reform, 1895–1912* (University of North Carolina Press, 1991), 181–84. Additional sources include the personal scrapbooks and original manuscripts of George Edmund Haynes.

p. 27 Early years at Fisk University: *The Catalogue of Fisk University*, 1899–1900, 73–74; and Perlman, *Stirring the White Conscience*, footnote 38.

p. 27 George Haynes' years at Fisk University: Earl Wright II, "The Tradition of Sociology at Fisk University," *Journal of African American Studies* 14, no. 1 (March 2010): 44–60.

p. 28 George Haynes' curriculum at Fisk University and his valedictory address: Samuel Kelton Roberts, *Crucible for a Vision: The Work of George Edmund Haynes and the Commission on Race Relations* (dissertation, Columbia University, 1974), 42–44.

p. 28 George Haynes's years at Yale University: Roberts, *Crucible for a Vision*, 55–58.

p. 28 Material on William Sumner: William Perdue, *Terrorism and the State: A Critique of Domination Through Fear* (Praeger Press, 1989), 5; and Carter A. Wilson, *Racism: From Slavery to Advanced Capitalism* (Sage Publications, 1997), 109–10.

p. 29 Haynes's education at Yale and Columbia and years with the YMCA: Ronald C. White Jr., *Liberty and Justice for All: Racial Reform and the Social Gospel (1877–1925)* (Westminster John Knox Press, 2002), 250–59; and Samuel K. Roberts, "George Edmund Haynes: Advocate for Interracial Cooperation," in *Black Apostles: Afro-American Clergy Confront the Twentieth Century*, ed. Randall K. Burkett and Richard Newman (G. K. Hall, 1978), 97–127. Pamela Bayless, *The YMCA at 150: The History of the YMCA of Greater New York 1852–2002* (Fordham University Press, 2002);

George Haynes's work with the YMCA: Randall K. Burkett and Richard Newman, eds., *Black Apostles: Afro-American Clergy Confront the Twentieth Century* (Boston: G. K. Hall & Co., 1978), 110–14.

p. 30   University of Chicago as a welcoming school for Negroes: Wilson, *Segregated Scholars*, 43–45.

p. 30   George Haynes, *The Negro at Work in New York City: A Study in Economic Progress* (dissertation, Columbia University, 1912).

p. 31   "More modern theories of migration exhibit remarkably little advance over Haynes' conception": James B. Stewart, "George Edmund Haynes and the Office of Negro Economics," in *A Different Vision: African American Economic Thought*, ed. Thomas D. Boston (Routledge, 1996), 1: 216–17.

p. 31   For more discussion on migration patterns and industrial jobs, see Gilbert Osofsky, *Harlem: The Making of a Ghetto* (Ivan R. Dee, 1996), 17–28.

p. 31   Haynes's contributions to sociology: Alford A. Young Jr. and Donald R. Deskins Jr., "Early Traditions of African-American Sociological Thought," *Annual Review of Sociology*, 27 (2001): 445–47.

p. 31   Correspondence between W. E. B. Du Bois and George Edmund Haynes: Wilson, *Segregated Scholars*, 64–65.

p. 31   Aldon D. Morris writes that Du Bois developed the first school of scientific sociology and that George Haynes—along with Monroe Work, Richard R. Wright Jr., and Mary Ovington—was part of the very first community of intellectuals that conceptualized race as socially constructed and "employed rigorous empirical methodologies" to back up their claims. See Morris, *The Scholar Denied: W. E. B. Du Bois and the Birth of Modern Sociology* (University of California Press, 2015).

p. 31   Founding of the National Urban League: L. Hollingsworth Wood, "The Urban League Movement," *Journal of Negro History* 9, no. 2 (April 1924): 117–26.

p. 31   George Haynes and the National Urban League: William R. Hutchinson, *Between the Times: The Travail of the Protest* (Cambridge University Press, 1990), 173–76.

p. 31   Early years of the National Urban League: E. E. Pratt, "Tribute to an Idea," in *National Urban League Fortieth Anniversary Yearbook*,

1950 (National Urban League, 1951), 6; and George Edmund Haynes, "Interracial Social Work Begins," in *National Urban League Fortieth Anniversary Yearbook*, 7.

p. 31   Early support for the National Urban League: John Louis Recchiuti, "Introduction: The Greatest Social Science Laboratory in the World," in *Civic Engagement: Social Science and Progressive-Era Reform in New York City* (University of Pennsylvania Press, 2007), 6; Wood, "The Urban League Movement," 117–26.

p. 32   Distinguishing the missions of the NAACP and the National Urban League: Recchiuti, *Civic Engagement*, 205.

p. 32   Mary White Ovington on the complementary strategies of the NAACP and the National Urban League: Benjamin L. Hooks and John E. Jacob, "Black Family Summit Conference to Convene May 3–5, 1984, at Fisk University, Nashville, Tennessee: Joint Statement of Purpose," *The Crisis* 91, no. 2 (64) (February 1984): 12.

p. 33   Du Bois's embrace of communism: In his application letter to the Communist Party USA, on October 1, 1961, Du Bois wrote, "Today I have reached my conclusion: Capitalism cannot reform itself; it is doomed to self-destruction. No universal selfishness can bring social goods to all." See Peter Kihss, "Dr. W. E. B. Du Bois Joins Communist Party at 93," *New York Times* (November 23, 1961).

p. 33   "More militant than Booker T. Washington but not as strident as W. E. B. Du Bois": Edgar Allan Toppin, "George Edmund Haynes," in *Africana: The Encyclopedia of the African and African-American Experience*, ed. Henry Louis Gates and Kwame Anthony Appiah (Oxford University Press, 2005), 186.

p. 34   Eugene Kinckle Jones's narrative on the National Urban League: Jones, "A Dream, A Quarter Century, A Reality! How the Urban League Has Served," *Opportunity Journal of Negro Life* 13, no. 11 (November 1935), http://newdeal.feri.org/opp/opp35328.htm.

p. 34   Background on Elizabeth Ross: James L. Conyers, *Black Lives: Essays in African American Biography* (M. E. Sharpe, 1998), 95–98; Wilson, *Segregated Scholars*; Gerda Lerner, ed., *Black Women in White America: A Documentary History* (Vintage, 1992), 255; and Paula J. Giddings, *When and Where I Enter: The Impact of Black Women on Race and Sex in America* (William Morrow, 1984).

p. 36   Occupational segregation and the financial vulnerability of middle-class families: Bruce Haynes, *Red Lines, Black Spaces: The*

Politics of Race and Space in a Black Middle-Class Suburb (Yale University Press, 2001), 14; Eric S. Brown, *The Black Professional Middle Class: Race, Class, and Community in the Post-Civil Right Era* (Routledge, 2014), 20; Bart Landry, *The New Black Middle Class* (University of California Press, 1988); and Gerald Jaynes and Robin Williams, eds., *A Common Destiny: Blacks and American Society* (National Academies Press, 1990).

p. 36   Career and marriage among black middle-class women: Bart Landry, *Black Working Wives: Pioneers of the American Family Revolution* (University of California Press, 2000), 64–75.

p. 36   Attitudes among black female social activists toward women in the workplace: Linda Gordon, "Black and White Visions of Welfare: Women's Welfare Activism, 1890–1945," *Journal of American History* (September 1991): 569, 584–87.

p. 36   "The economic independence that will some day enable them to make their place in the ranks with other working women": "Negroes in Domestic Service in the United States," *Journal of Negro History* 8, no. 4 (October 1923): 384–442, cited in Conyers, *Black Lives*, 107.

p. 37   On black female social reformers: The sociologist Bart Landry argues that black middle-class women advanced a "new feminist ideology" that embraced egalitarianism within the home and a more active role outside the home, and that economic need alone cannot explain their tendency to pursue careers. See Landry, *Black Working Wives*, 83.

p. 37   "Hang over training to shove [men] forward instead of ourselves": Iris Carlton-LaNey, "Elizabeth Ross Haynes: An African American Reformer of Womanist Consciousness, 1980–1940," in *The Womanist Reader: The First Quarter of Womanist Thought*, ed. Layli Phillips (Routledge, 2006), 305.

p. 37   The *Negro Motorist Green Book* was a travel guide series published from 1936 to 1966 by Victor H. Green, a postal worker, to help Negro motorists and tourists find lodging and dining that would accommodate them.

p. 37   Lynching of Jesse and William Powell: Ralph Ginzburg, *100 Years of Lynchings* (Black Classic Press, 1996), 254.

p. 38   Black migration during the war years: James R. Grossman, ed., *Black Workers in the Era of the Great Migration, 1916–1929* (University

Publications of America, 1985), vii; and Felix L. Armfield, *Eugene Kinckle Jones: The National Urban League and Black Social Work, 1910–1940* (University of Illinois Press, 2001), 24–27.

p. 38   Role of the *Chicago Defender* in spurring migration of blacks to the North: William G. Jordan, *Black Newspapers and America's War for Democracy: 1914–1920* (University of North Carolina Press, 2001), 33.

p. 38   East Saint Louis race riot: Harper Barnes, *Never Been a Time: The 1917 Race Riot That Sparked the Civil Rights Movement* (Walker Books, 2008); and Charles Lumpkins, *American Pogrom: The East St. Louis Race Riot and Black Politics* (Ohio University Press, 2008).

p. 38   Events leading to the Division of Negro Economics: Robert H. Zieger, "Grudgingly, Unwillingly, Almost Insultingly: Racial Progress in the Era of the Great War" (2008), http://www.bu.edu/historic/conference08/rzieger.pdf; and Roberts, *Crucible for a Vision*, 66–68.

p. 39   On Giles Jackson, "one of the most disreputable characters the Negro race has produced": Henry Guzda, "Labor Department's First Program to Assist Black Workers," *Monthly Labor Review* 105 (June 1982): 40. Du Bois considered Jackson a tool of the Jim Crow South. He wrote, "I want to get the exact facts in the career of Giles Jackson. He is becoming to be a dangerous catspaw in the hands of the South. We must expose him. How can I get the facts?" W. E. B. Du Bois to Reverend James R. L. Diggs, April 19, 1918, Special Collections and University Archives, University of Massachusetts Amherst Libraries, MS 312, http://oubliette.library.umass.edu/view/pageturn/mums312-b011-i202/#page/1/mode/1up.

p. 39   Elizabeth Ross Haynes working alongside George Haynes as assistant director of the Division of Negro Economics and as a "dollar-a-year" worker for the department's Women in Industry Service: Barbara Sicherman and Carol Hurd Green, eds., *Notable American Women, A Biographical Dictionary*, vol. 4, *The Modern Period* (Belknap Press of Harvard University Press, 1986).

p. 39   Segregationist policies under Woodrow Wilson: Eric S. Yellin, *Racism in the Nation's Service: Government Workers and the Color Line in Woodrow Wilson's America* (University of North Carolina Press, 2016).

p. 40   Haynes's years at U.S. Department of Labor: Guzda, "Labor Department's First Program."

p. 40   Haynes's contributions to social economic thought: James B. Stewart, "The Rise and Fall of Negro Economics: The Economic Thought of George Edmund Haynes," *American Economic Review* 81, no. 2 (May 1991).

p. 41   "Boll-weavil in de cotton": George Edmund Haynes, "The Negroes Move North," *Survey* (May 4, 1918): 120.

p. 41   Red Summer of 1919: Jan Voogd, *Race Riots and Resistance: The Red Summer of 1919* (Peter Lang, 2008); Cameron McWhirter, *Red Summer: The Summer of 1919 and the Awakening of Black America* (Henry Holt, 2011); and Arthur E. Barbeau and Florette Henri, *The Unknown Soldiers: African-American Troops in World War I* (Temple University Press, 1996), 175–89.

p. 41   George Haynes, "What Negroes Think of the Race Riots," *The Public: A Journal of Democracy* 22 (August 9, 1919): 848–49.

p. 41   Harlem's 15th New York National Guard Regiment: David Levering Lewis, *When Harlem Was in Vogue* (Penguin, 1997), 3–5; and Jill Watts, *God, Harlem USA: The Father Divine Story* (University of California Press, 1992), 49.

p. 42   "The Negro Voter on Election Day," cited in its entirety with permission: Barry Singer, *Black and Blue: The Life and Lyrics of Andy Razaf* (Schirmer Books, 1992), 51.

p. 42   Waning support for Division of Negro Economics: Guzda, "Labor Department's First Program," 43–44.

3. NEW NEGROES

p. 45   Harlem during Prohibition: Chad Heap, *Slumming: Sexual and Racial Encounters in American Nightlife: 1885–1940* (University of Chicago Press, 2000), 189, 211.

p. 45   Harlem's "whites-only" jazz clubs of the 1920s: Burton W. Peretti, *Nightclub City: Politics and Amusement in Manhattan* (University of Pennsylvania, 2007), 19–22.

p. 46   "Slum boom" and Harlem rents: Gilbert Osofsky, *Harlem: The Making of a Ghetto* (Ivan R. Dee, 1996), 136.

p. 47   Housing congestion and mortality rate in Harlem: James Trager, *The New York Chronology: The Ultimate Compendium of Events, People, and Anecdotes from the Dutch to the Present* (HarperCollins, 2003), 442; and Gail Radford, *Modern Housing for America: Policy*

Struggles in the New Deal Era (University of Chicago Press, 1997), 149–50.

p. 47   Segregated hiring practices at Macy's and Gimbels department stores: Osofsky, *Harlem: The Making of a Ghetto*, 136–37; and Roderick D. Bush, *We Are Not What We Seem: Black Nationalism and Class Struggle in the American Century* (New York University Press, 2000), 121.

p. 47   Segregated hiring practices at Blumstein's department store in Harlem: Maurianne Adams, *Strangers and Neighbors: Relations Between Blacks and Jews in the United States* (University of Massachusetts Press, 2000), 412.

p. 47   "Not because of any prejudice on the part of the company . . .": *Pittsburgh Courier* (May 10, 1930): 12; Osofsky, *Harlem: The Making of a Ghetto*, 137.

p. 47   Movement of blacks into Harlem in the 1920s: E. Franklin Frazier, "Negro Harlem: An Ecological Study," *American Journal of Sociology* 43, no. 1 (July 1937), 72–88.

p. 47   Harlem associations, clubs, societies, churches, and institutions: Osofsky, *Harlem: The Making of a Ghetto*, 132.

p. 48   "Our poets have now stopped speaking for the Negro": Alain Locke, "Youth Speaks," *Survey Graphic* 6, no. 6 (March 1925): 659.

p. 48   Depictions of Negroes in children's literature: Rudine Sims Bishop, "Give Them Back Their Own Souls," in *Free Within Ourselves: The Development of African American Children's Literature* (Greenwood, 2007); David Pilgrim, *Understanding Jim Crow: Using Racist Memorabilia to Teach Tolerance and Promote Social Justice* (PM Press, 2015); and Barbara Bader, "Sambo, Babaji, and Sam," *The Horn Book Magazine* 72, no. 5 (September–October 1996): 536.

p. 49   Description of Topsy: Harriet Beecher Stowe, *Uncle Tom's Cabin* (New American Library, 1966), 258.

p. 49   Elizabeth Haynes, *Unsung Heroes* (Du Bois and Dill, 1921).

p. 49   Mission of *The Brownies' Book*: Donald F. Joyce, *Black Book Publishers in the United States: A Historical Dictionary of the Presses, 1817–1990* (Greenwood Publishing Group, 1991), 93–96; and W. E. B. Du Bois, "Opinion of W. E. B. Du Bois," *The Crisis* 18, no. 6 (October 1919).

p. 49   Early black publishers: Donald F. Joyce, *Black Book Publishers*, 93–96; and Violet J. Harris, "*The Brownies' Book*: Challenge to the

Selective Tradition in Children's Literature," *Viewpoints* 120 (1984).

p. 49 Langston Hughes on Elizabeth Haynes's *Unsung Heroes*: Hughes, "Books and the Negro Child," *Children's Library Yearbook* 4 (1932): 108–10.

p. 51 Commission on Negro Churches and Race Relations for the Federal Council of Churches and its emphasis on the Negro arts: Samuel Kelton Roberts, *Crucible for a Vision: The Work of George Edmund Haynes and the Commission on Race Relations* (dissertation, Columbia University, 1974), 258.

p. 51 Harmon Foundation awards: Mary Ann Calo, *Distinction and Denial: Race, Nation, and the Critical Construction of the African American Artist, 1920–40* (University of Michigan Press, 2007), 115–32.

p. 51 Harlem Renaissance writers and artists: David Levering Lewis, *When Harlem Was in Vogue* (Penguin, 1997).

p. 51 Countee Cullen to George Haynes, December 7, 1926, Harmon Foundation Records, Manuscript Division, 7–10, courtesy of the Countee Cullen Papers, Amistad Research Center, Tulane University, New Orleans, Louisiana.

p. 52 Discussion of black stereotypes in American literature of the nineteenth and twentieth centuries: Sterling Brown, "The Negro Character as Seen by White Authors," *Journal of Negro Education* 2, no. 2 (April 1933).

p. 52 Relationship between George Haynes and T. S. Stribling: Kenneth W. Vickers, *T. S. Stribling: A Life of the Tennessee Novelist* (University of Tennessee Press, 2003), 69–70, 77, 80, 88–93, 95, 203–4.

p. 53 The Scottsboro Boys: Mark Naison, *Communists in Harlem During the Depression* (University of Illinois Press, 2005), 57–89.

p. 53 Haynes's involvement in the Scottsboro case: Dan T. Carter, *Scottsboro: A Tragedy of the American South* (Louisiana State University, 1969), 316–17, 335–37; Naison, *Communists in Harlem*, 129–34; and Shelton Hale Bishop to George Haynes, November 1, 1934, ILD Papers, Reel 3, C 48, cited in Naison, *Communists in Harlem*, 160.

p. 54 Du Bois's embrace of Marxism and his shift from racial integration: Manning Marable, *W. E. B. Du Bois: Black Radical Democrat* (Paradigm, 1986), 136–43.

p. 54   Pan-African Congress movement: Marable, *W. E. B. Du Bois*, 99–120.

p. 54   Haynes's involvement in the Pan-African Congress movement: Haynes expressed support for the 1921 Pan-African Congress and provided names of potential invitees. See George Haynes to W. E. B. Du Bois, March 10, 1921, Special Collections and University Archives, University of Massachusetts Amherst Libraries, 2 pages, http://credo.library.umass.edu/view/pageturn/mums312 -b017-i243/#page/1/mode/1up, and http://credo.library.umass .edu/view/pageturn/mums312-b017-i244/#page/1/mode/1up.

p. 54   Haynes on the New Deal and exclusion of blacks from social security programs: George Haynes, "Open Fight to Make Security Act Safe for All U.S. Citizens," *Chicago Defender* (February 2, 1935); and Haynes, "Lily-White Social Security," *The Crisis* (March 1935): 85–86.

p. 55   Harlem Riot of 1935: After the riot, Mayor Fiorello Henry La Guardia appointed a twelve-member biracial commission, which included the poet Countee Cullen, the sociologist Asa Philip Randolph, and E. Franklin, the leading sociologist of the era. The report identified social and economic conditions that fed tensions leading to the riot. The report's indictment of police brutality and general lack of courtesy to the Negro public encouraged La Guardia to bury the report.

p. 55   For ongoing correspondence between George Haynes and W. E. B. Du Bois, see the Special Collections and University Archives, University of Massachusetts Amherst Libraries, http://credo.library .umass.edu.

p. 56   Numbers of black men serving in combat in World War II: National Bureau of Economic Research, "The GI Bill, World War II, and the Education of Black Americans," http://www.nber.org /digest/dec02/w9044.html.

p. 56   For more on the Buffalo Soldiers, see Hondon B. Hargrove, *Buffalo Soldiers in Italy: Black Americans in World War II* (McFarland Publishers, 2003).

p. 56   Segregation in the U.S. Army during World War II: Rawn James Jr., *The Double V: How Wars, Protest, and Harry Truman Desegregated America's Military* (Bloomsbury Press, 2014), 166, 173–74.

p. 57   Exclusion of blacks from jobs in the defense industry: John White and Bruce J. Dierenfield, *History of African-American Leadership* (Routledge, 2014), 125; Walter Hazen, *American Black History* (Milliken Publishing, 2004), 55–56; and Henry Louis Taylor Jr. and Walter Hill, eds., *Historical Roots of the Urban Crisis: African Americans in the Industrial City, 1900–1950* (Garland Publishing, 2000), 236–40.

p. 57   Rise of black left in 1940s and coalition building to dismantle segregation: Martha Biondi, *To Stand and Fight: The Struggle for Civil Rights in Postwar New York City* (Harvard University Press, 2003), 7; and Naison, *Communists in Harlem*, 198–99. International events in the late 1930s had already moved many black intellectuals to the left—in support of Ethiopia, against the Italian fascists, and for the Spanish loyalists against right-wing military forces during the Spanish Civil War.

p. 57   A. Philip Randolph threatened a March on Washington: Naison, *Communists in Harlem*, 310–11.

p. 58   Black engineers in the 1940s: Amy E. Slaton, *Race, Rigor, and U.S. Engineering: The History of an Occupational Color Line* (Harvard University Press, 2010), 49–52.

p. 58   "Ill-prepared not just educationally, but psychologically and even morally, for scientific careers": Slaton, *Race, Rigor, and U.S. Engineering*, 52.

p. 58   Although few black engineers were employed in the private sphere during the 1940s, the Fort Monmouth, New Jersey, army post, a major center of electronic development for the U.S. Army, employed minority scientists, engineers, and technologists. See Patricia Carter Sluby, *The Inventive Spirit of African Americans: Patented Ingenuity* (Praeger Press, 2004), 176.

p. 58   Black professionals and semiprofessionals in 1930: Carter G. Woodson, cited in Bart Landry, *The New Black Middle Class* (University of California Press, 1988), 52.

p. 59   Lodges and fraternal societies have long been a part of American history. But the color line produced Prince Hall Freemasonry, the black offshoot of white Freemasonry in America, as well as Order of the Eastern Star, the black women's auxiliary group. Largely middle class, Prince Hall Masons and the Eastern Stars were civically engaged and active in the early civil rights struggle. See William Alan Muraskin, *Middle-Class Blacks in a White Society: Prince Hall Masonry in America* (University of California Press, 1976); and Bruce Haynes, *Red Lines, Black Spaces: The Politics of Race and Space in a Black Middle-Class Suburb* (Yale University Press, 2001), 95–96.

p. 61   W. E. B. Du Bois and Shirley Graham to George E. Haynes, October 27, 1953 (on the death of Elizabeth Haynes), Special Collections and University Archives, University of Massachusetts Amherst Libraries, MS 312, http://credo.library.umass.edu/view /full/mums312-b140-i122; and to Dr. and Mrs. George Edmund Haynes, April 27, 1955 (on the marriage to Olyve Jeter Haynes), Special Collections, MS 312, http://credo.library.umass.edu/view /full/mums312-b143-i409.

p. 62   United States Census Bureau, "New York—Race and Hispanic Origin for Selected Large Cities and Other Places: Earliest Census to 1990," www.census.gov/population/www /documentation/twps0076/NYtab.pdf; City of New York, "Part A–Population, New York City," https://www1.nyc.gov/assets/doh /downloads/pdf/tb/tb1967-other.pdf.

4. SOUL DOLLARS

p. 65   Neighborhoods of Harlem: Bruce D. Haynes, "In Terms of Harlem," in *The Ghetto: Contemporary Global Issues and Controversies*, ed. Ray Hutchison and Bruce D. Haynes (Westview Press, 2011), 111–35.

p. 70   Arrest of Mamie Canty: Shawn G. Kennedy, "Six Are Arrested on Drug Charges: Harlem Ring Called Broken," *New York Times* (April 2, 1983): 38.

p. 72   Higher prices charged to poor people: David Caplovitz, *The Poor Pay More: Consumer Practices of Low-Income Families* (Free Press, 1967).

p. 72   Segregation in New York City schools in the 1960s: Jerald E. Podair, *The Strike That Changed New York: Blacks, Whites, and the Ocean Hill–Brownsville Crisis* (Yale University Press, 2002), 16–17.

p. 72   "Combat pay" to attract experienced teachers to black schools: Podair, *The Strike*, 16.

p. 72   Black children in New York's public schools read on average two grade levels below their white counterparts: Podair, *The Strike*, 17.

p. 74   New York City teachers strike: Podair, *The Strike*, 113–14; Diane Ravitch, *The Great School Wars: A History of the New York City Public Schools* (Johns Hopkins University Press), 2000; Vincent J. Cannato, *The Ungovernable City: John Lindsay and His Struggle to Save New York* (Basic Books, 2001), 301–52; Daniel Perlstein, "Community Control of Schools," in *Encyclopedia of African American Education*, ed. Kofi Lomotey (Sage 2010), 1:180–82; Nancy A. Naples, *Feminism and Method: Ethnography, Discourse Analysis, and Activist Research* (Routledge, 2003); and McGeorge Bundy, *Reconnection for Learning: A Community School System for New York City* (Praeger, 1967).

p. 75   Demise of P.S. 186: Mirela Iverac, "Anger and Debate in Harlem over What to Do With a Long-Vacant School," *New York Times* (August 2, 2010); and Erin Durkin, "Long-Vacant Harlem School Site Moves Toward Development," *New York Sun* (July 12, 2007).

5. STEPPING OUT

p. 82   Lewis Michaux: Peter Goldman, *The Death and Life of Malcolm X* (University of Illinois Press, 1979), 51, 377; Hugh Pearson, *When Harlem Nearly Killed King* (Seven Stories Press, 2002), 40–45; Charlayne Hunter, "Lull," *New Yorker* (November 11, 1956); Hunter, "The Professor," *New Yorker* (September 3, 1966); and interviews with the author's brother George Haynes.

p. 83   Black art and Black Power: Larry Neal wrote, "The Black Arts Movement is radically opposed to any concept of the artist that alienates him from his community. This movement is the aesthetic and spiritual sister of the Black Power concept." Neal, "The Black Arts Movement" (1968), reprinted in National Humanities Center, *The Making of African American Identity*, vol. 3, 1917–1968, http://nationalhumanitiescenter.org/pds/maai3/community/text8/blackartsmovement.pdf.

p. 83   Poor People's Campaign of 1968: Gwendolyn Mink and Alice M. O'Connor, eds., *Poverty in the United States: An Encyclopedia of History, Politics, and Policy* (ABC-CLIO, 2004), 2:556.

p. 85 Black liberation flag and its origins: Tony Martin, *Race First: The Ideological and Organizational Struggles of Marcus Garvey and the Universal Negro Improvement Association* (Greenwood Press, 1987), 43–44.

p. 87 John L. Jackson Jr., *Harlemworld: Doing Race and Class in Contemporary Black America* (University of Chicago Press, 2003).

p. 87 On West Indian culture and success: Thomas Sowell, *Ethnic America* (Basic Books, 1981), 220.

p. 87 West Indian exceptionalism: Bruce Haynes, *Red Lines, Black Spaces: The Politics of Race and Space in a Black Middle-Class Suburb* (Yale University Press, 2001), 47–49; and Stephen Steinberg, *The Ethnic Myth: Race, Ethnicity, and Class in America*, 3rd ed. (Beacon Press, 2001), 275–80.

p. 91 Whitney Young's call for a domestic "Marshall Plan": Molefi Kete Asante and Mambo Ama Mazama, eds., *Encyclopedia of Black Studies* (Sage, 2004), 367; Laura Warren Hill and Julia Rabig, eds., *The Business of Black Power: Community Development, Capitalism, and Corporate Responsibility in Postwar America* (University of Rochester Press, 2012), 24–25; and Daniel Geary, *Beyond Civil Rights: The Moynihan Report and Its Legacy* (University of Pennsylvania Press, 2015), 45.

p. 91 Changes to National Urban League under Whitney Young: Thomas F. Jackson, "The State, the Movement, and the Urban Poor: The War on Poverty and Political Mobilization in the 1960s," in *The "Underclass" Debate*, ed. Michael B. Katz (Princeton University Press, 1992), 431.

p. 91 Growth of National Urban League under Whitney Young: Nancy Joan Weiss, *Whitney M. Young, Jr., and the Struggle for Civil Rights* (Princeton University Press, 2014), 97.

p. 91 Whitney Young and 1963 March on Washington: William H. Chafe, *The Unfinished Journey: America Since World War II* (Oxford University Press, 2002), 302; and Paul Finkelman, *Encyclopedia of African American History, 1896 to the Present: From the Age of Segregation to the Twenty-First Century* (Oxford University Press, 2009), 400.

p. 92 Federal and foundation funding of the National Urban League under Whitney Young: Herbert H. Haines, "Black Radicalization and the Funding of Civil Rights: 1957–1970," *Social Problems* 32, no. 1 (October 1984): 31–43.

p. 92   1964 Harlem Riot: Walter C. Rucker and James N. Upton, eds., *Encyclopedia of American Race Riots* (Greenwood Press, 2007), 2:478–79.

p. 96   Floyd McKissick and Soul City: Brentin Mock, "The Time Republicans Helped Build an All-Black Town Called 'Soul City,'" *CityLab* (November 6, 2015), http://www.citylab.com/politics/2015/11/the-time-republicans-helped-build-an-all-black-town-called-soul-city/414585; and Christopher B. Strain, "Soul City, North Carolina and the Business of Black Power," in *The Economic Civil Rights Movement: African Americans and the Struggle for Economic Power*, ed. Michael Ezra (Routledge, 2013), 188–201.

p. 97   Findings on disadvantaged women admitted to CUNY in the early 1970s: Paul Attewell and David E. Lavin, *Passing the Torch: Does Higher Education for the Disadvantaged Pay Off Across the Generations?* (Russell Sage Foundation, 2007).

p. 97   Leonard Bernstein's dinner party for the Black Panthers: Tom Wolfe, "Radical Chic: That Party at Lenny's," *New York* (June 8, 1970).

6. DO FOR YOURSELF

p. 100   Bensalem College: John Coyne, "Bensalem: When the Dream Died," *Change* 4, no. 8 (October 1972): 39–44; James McCabe, "Radical Departure from the '70s: History of Bensalem," *Inside Ford University* 21 (Fall 2005); Judson Jerome, "Friends World College, Bensalem, the College of the Potomac: Portrait of Three Experiments," *Change* (July–August 1970); and "A Look at Bensalem College," *Look* (May 19, 1970).

p. 100   New York School of Ethical Culture: William Chamberlin Hunt, *Religious Bodies: 1916* (United States Bureau of the Census, 1919).

p. 105   Savior letter to join the Nation of Islam: Richard Brent Turner, *Islam in the African-American Experience* (Indiana University Press, 2003), 188; and Martha Lee, *The Nation of Islam: An American Millenarian Movement* (Syracuse University Press, 1996), 37.

p. 108   Nation of Islam fish business: Interview with George Haynes III, June 2011; and Edward E. Curtis IV, *Black Muslim Religion in the Nation of Islam* (University of North Carolina Press, 2007), 105.

p. 109   Wealth and investments of Nation of Islam: Laurence Mamiya, "African American Muslims," in *Encyclopedia of Muslim-American*

History (Facts on File, 2008); Ernest Allen Jr., "Religious Hetero-doxy and Nationalist Tradition: The Continuing Evolution of the Nation of Islam," *Black Scholar* 26, no. 3–4: 15; and Curtis, *Black Muslim Religion in the Nation of Islam*, 102–105.

p. 109 Other background on the Nation of Islam: Hans A. Baer and Merrill Singer, *African-American Religion in the Twentieth Century* (University of Tennessee Press, 1992); E. U. Essien-Udom, *Black Nationalism: A Search for an Identity in America* (University of Chicago Press, 1962); and Curtis, *Black Muslim Religion in the Nation of Islam* (dietary restrictions, 98–102; Fruit of Islam, 136–38; University of Islam and youth education, 153–55).

p. 111 On the "man in the house" rule, the 1968 Supreme Court decision striking it down, and Aid to Families with Dependent Children penalties against intact families: Barbara Bergmann, *The Economic Emergence of Women* (Palgrave Macmillan, 2005), 164; and R. Shep Melnick, *Between the Lines: Interpreting Welfare Rights* (Brookings Institution Press, 1994), 83–98.

7. FREE FALL

p. 113 New York City's poverty rate from 1970 to 1980: John F. McDonald, *Urban America: Growth, Crisis, and Rebirth* (M. E. Sharpe, 2008), 156–57.

p. 113 Figures on New York's declining population in the 1970s: Andrew Karmen, *New York Murder Mystery: A True Story Behind the Crime Crash of the 1990s* (New York University Press, 2000), 232.

p. 114 Fiscal strains on New York City: McDonald, *Urban America*, 158.

p. 114 "You don't give her $100 a day": Felix G. Rohatyn, *Dealings: A Political and Financial Life* (Simon & Schuster, 2010), 124.

p. 114 Figures on sentencing of convicts: Karmen, *New York Murder Mystery*, 144–45, citing M. Patterson, "The Violent Get Easier Bail: Study," *Daily News* (February 14, 1978).

p. 115 "No, it was not a decade for the dainty": James Wolcott, "Splendor in the Grit," *Vanity Fair* (June 2009).

p. 115 For discussion of postwar industrial decline and the rise in con-centrated urban black poverty, see William Julius Wilson, *The Truly Disadvantaged: The Inner City, the Underclass, and Public Policy* (University of Chicago Press, 1990).

p. 115 For discussion of transfer of federal resources from the cities to the suburbs, see David M. P. Freund, "Marketing the Free Market: State Intervention and the Politics of Prosperity in Metropolitan America," in *The New Suburban History*, ed. Kevin M. Kruse and Thomas J. Sugrue (University of Chicago Press, 2006).

p. 115 For discussion of the role of housing discrimination in perpetuating hypersegregation, see Douglas S. Massey and Nancy A. Denton, *American Apartheid: Segregation and the Making of the Underclass* (Harvard University Press, 1990).

p. 115 George Haynes on segregation in 1913: George E. Haynes, "Conditions Among Negroes in the City," *Annals of the American Academy of Political and Social Science* 49 (September 1913).

p. 116 Criminal justice system in New York: Karmen, *New York Murder Mystery*, 144.

p. 116 Randy Young, "Dodge City, the Deadliest Precinct in Town," *New York* (August 28, 1978): 43–48.

p. 116 System-wide corruption: Knapp Commission (1972) findings, cited in Karmen, *New York Murder Mystery*, 164.

p. 116 Police corruption in Harlem (including Knapp Commission and William Phillips quotes): T. J. English, *Savage City: Race, Murder, and a Generation on the Edge* (HarperCollins, 2011), 86–88, 122–25, 160–64, 346; and Leonard Schecter, with William Phillips, *On the Pad: The Underworld and Its Corrupt Police, the Confessions of a Cop on the Take* (Putnam, 1973).

p. 117 Sentencing of William Phillips: Thomas J. Lueck, "Officer Jailed for 32 Years Wins Parole," *New York Times* (September 23, 2007).

p. 118 Dirty 30 and the Mollen Commission Report: *Commission to Investigate Allegations of Police Corruption and the Anti-Corruption Procedures of the Police Department Commission Report* (July 7, 1994), https://www.scribd.com/document/248581606/1994-07-07-Mollen-Commission-NYPD-Report; and Eric Pooley, "Untouchable," *New York* (July 11, 1994).

p. 119 Racially restrictive covenants and development of suburban communities: Kenneth T. Jackson, *Crabgrass Frontier: Suburbanization in the United States* (Oxford University Press, 1985).

p. 119 Shifting demographics and economic collapse of the South Bronx: Evelyn Gonzalez, *The Bronx* (Columbia University Press, 2003), 109–29.

p. 120   Data on standing housing units and population in the South Bronx: McDonald, *Urban America*, 157; John F. McDonald, *Postwar Urban America: Demography, Economics, and Social Policies* (Routledge, 2015), 137.

p. 120   South Bronx arson and homicide: Jim Rooney, *Organizing the South Bronx* (SUNY Press, 1994), 56–57; and Harold DeRiezo, *The Concept of Community: Lessons from the Bronx* (Ipoc Press, 2008), 198.

p. 120   Gangs in South Bronx in the 1970s: Eric C. Schneider, *Vampires, Dragons, and Egyptian Kings: Youth Gangs in Postwar New York* (Princeton University Press, 1999), 238–45.

p. 131   Early cable television channels in New York City: Leah Churner, posts on the Museum of the Moving Image website, including "The Poor Soul of Television" (June 25, 2009), http://www.mov ingimagesource.us/articles/the-poor-soul-of-television-20090625; "Un-TV: Public Access Cable Television in Manhattan: An Oral History" (February 10, 2011), http://www.movingimagesource.us /articles/un-tv-20110210; and "Out of the Vast Wasteland: The Early Years of Public Access Cable Television in New York City" (June 18, 2009), http://www.movingimagesource.us/articles/out-of-the-vast -wasteland-20090618.

p. 132   Ansonia Hotel: Steven Gaines, "The Building of the Upper West Side," *New York*, May 21, 2005; and Mary K. Fons, "Inside the Ansonia," *The Cooperator: The Co-op & Condo Monthly* (September 2005).

p. 136   42nd Street in the 1970s: Interviews with George Haynes, June 2011; Anthony Bianco, *Ghosts of 42nd Street: A History of America's Most Infamous Block* (Harper Perennial, 2005), 168–71, 208, 250, 242–43; Josh Alan Friedman, *Tales of Times Square* (Delacorte, 1986), 63–82; and James Traub, *The Devil's Playground: A Century of Pleasure and Profit in Times Square* (Random House, 2004), 119–21, 191–93.

8. MOVING ON DOWN

p. 145   Low earnings of street-level drug dealers: Steven D. Levitt and Sudhir Alladi Venkatesh, "An Economic Analysis of a Drug-Selling Gang's Finances," *Quarterly Journal of Economics* 115, no. 3 (August 2000): 755–89; and Steven D. Levitt and Stephen J. Dubner, *Freakonomics: A Rogue Economist Explores the Hidden Side of Everything* (HarperCollins, 2005).

p. 148   Nixon and the "War on Drugs": In a June 17, 1971, press conference, President Richard Nixon declared, "America's public enemy
number one in the United States is drug abuse. In order to fight
and defeat this enemy, it is necessary to wage a new, all-out offensive." In 1973, he announced that his administration had "declared
all-out, global war on the drug menace." See Richard M. Nixon,
"Remarks About an Intensified Program for Drug Abuse Pre-
vention and Control," in *Public Papers of the Presidents: Richard
Nixon, 1971* (United States Government Printing Office, 1972),
738; and Nixon, "Message to the Congress Transmitting Reorga-
nization Plan 2 of 1973 Establishing the Drug Enforcement Administration" (March 28, 1973), American Presidency Project, http://
www.presidency.ucsb.edu/ws/?pid=4159. In 1970, sociologist Troy
Duster prophesied the social condemnation and stigmatization of
drug use among America's "vulnerable" classes and showed that
legislation could moralize and stigmatize social behavior. Duster,
The Legislation of Morality: Law, Drugs, and Moral Judgment (Free
Press, 1970).

p. 149   The Anti–Drug Abuse Act of 1986 mandated severe minimum
sentences for drug dealers, with especially high sentences for those
who dealt crack cocaine. One would need around eighteen ounces
(a small suitcase full) of powdered cocaine to trigger the same
mandatory minimum prison term as that imposed on a person with
a few pebble-size "rocks" that a child could hold in one hand—and
this came without any possibility of parole or sentence suspension.
Because 86 percent of crack users were black, the law had a devastating effect on black urban communities. See Gail Winger, James
H. Woods, and Frederick G. Hofmann, *A Handbook on Drug and
Alcohol Abuse: The Biomedical Aspects*, 4th ed. (Oxford University
Press, 2004), 162.

p. 149   Khalil Gibran Muhammad, *The Condemnation of Blackness* (Harvard University Press, 2011) details the ways in which criminality
has been linked to race. While white people may "commit crimes,"
black men have been defined as "criminal." This criminalization
of black men took on a new power with the 1986 Anti–Drug Abuse
Act, which imposed harsher sentences for distribution of crack—
seen as a "black" drug—than for powder cocaine, which was associated with whites. Berkeley sociologist Loic Wacquant argues

that, in the life course of today's African Americans, the plantation has simply been supplemented by the prison. See Wacquant, "From Slavery to Mass Incarceration: Rethinking the 'Race Question' in the US," *New Left Review* 13 (January–February 2000): 41–60. In 2003, Angela Davis published her prophetic book *Are Prisons Obsolete?* (Seven Stories Press), in which she argues that prisons have become warehouses where capitalist interests are at work. Sociologists Bruce Western and Becky Pettit show that black men who were born between 1965 and 1969 had a far higher risk of being incarcerated than their white counterparts, and that those risks were further stratified by education. Sixty percent of black high school dropouts and 30 percent of those without a college education would go to prison by 1999. See Western and Pettit, "Mass Imprisonment and the Life Course: Race and Class Inequality in U.S. Incarceration," *American Sociological Review* 69, no. 2 (April 2004): 151–69. Most recently, Michelle Alexander showed that there are more blacks in prison today than there were blacks in slavery at the end of Reconstruction. See Alexander, *The New Jim Crow: Mass Incarceration in the Age of Color Blindness* (The New Press, 2012).

p. 149 Spending on prisons and drug treatment: Beverly Xaviera Watkins and Mindy Thompson Fullilove, "Crack Cocaine and Harlem's Health," *Souls* (Winter 1999): 39.

p. 149 Introduction of cocaine extraction kit at New York's fashion week: Edith Fairman Cooper, *Emergence of Crack Cocaine Abuse* (Nova Science, 2002), 88.

p. 152 Emergence of crack cocaine: Jill Jonnes, *Hep-Cats, Narcs, and Pipe Dreams: A History of America's Romance with Illegal Drugs* (Johns Hopkins University Press, 1999), 367–88; and John P. Morgan and Lynn Zimmer, "The Social Pharmacology of Smokeable Cocaine," in *Crack in America: Demon Drugs and Social Justice*, ed. Craig Reinarman and Harry G. Levine (University of California Press, 1997), 131–55.

p. 153 Pyramidology: Erik Hornung, *The Secret Lore of Egypt: Its Impact on the West* (Cornell University Press, 2001).

p. 156 Deinstitutionalization of the mentally ill: Alexander Thomas, "Ronald Reagan and the Commitment of the Mentally Ill: Capital, Interest Groups, and the Eclipse of Social Policy," *Electronic Journal of Sociology* (1998), http://sociology.org/content/vol003.004/thomas_d.html; Arline Mathieu, "The Medicalization of Homelessness and the Theater of Repression," *Medical Anthropology Quarterly* 7, no. 2 (June 1993): 170–84; William G. Rothstein, ed., *Readings in American Health Care: Current Issues in Socio-Historical Perspective* (University of Wisconsin Press, 1995), 290–91; and Russell K. Schutt and Stephen M. Goldfinger, *Homelessness, Housing, and Mental Illness* (Harvard University Press, 2011), 47–49.

p. 156 Willowbrook State School was a children's school for the severely mentally disabled (then called the "mentally retarded") in Staten Island, New York. Conditions were so deplorable that, by the 1960s, most newly admitted children would contract hepatitis. See Saul Krugman, "The Willowbrook Hepatitis Studies Revisited: Ethical Aspects," *Reviews of Infectious Diseases* 8, no. 1 (January/February 1986): 156–62. In 1972, *Eyewitness News* correspondent Geraldo Rivera gained access to one of the school's buildings and filmed graphic scenes of rampant neglect, including feces-smeared walls and naked children. His exposé led to federal lawsuits and the school's eventual closure.

p. 159 Jury selection and Jay Schulman: Alan M. Goldstein and Irving B. Weiner, eds., *Handbook of Psychology*, vol. 11, *Forensic Psychology* (Wiley, 2003), 167–72; and Keith Devlin and Gary Lorden, *The Numbers Behind NUMB3RS: Solving Crime with Mathematics* (Plume, 2007).

p. 160 "There's no point in raising children if they're going to be burned alive": "Quick, Go Get Dr. Spock," *Life* (December 14, 1962): 90–92A.

p. 160 Bias in jury pool for Dr. Spock trial: Devlin and Lorden, *The Numbers Behind NUMB3RS*, 190.

p. 161 Jury selection and the Harrisburg Seven: Margaret Bull Kovera and Brian L. Cutler, *Jury Selection (Guides to Best Practices for Forensic Mental Health Assessment)* (Oxford University Press, 2012), 31–32.

p. 163 Charles Hynes's firsthand account of the Howard Beach trial: Charles J. Hynes and Bob Drury, *Incident at Howard Beach: The Case for Murder* (Putnam Adult, 1990), 208–9.

9. KEEP ON KEEPIN' ON

p. 165 Upper Manhattan Empowerment Zone: Sharon Zukin, *Naked City: The Death and Life of Authentic Urban Places* (Oxford University Press, 2010), 79.

p. 175 Although Archer Avenue is the fictional setting of Wes Anderson's *The Royal Tenenbaums*, the actual location of the film was 339 Convent Avenue, an eight-thousand-square-foot home at the corner of Convent Avenue and 144th Street. Tom McGeveran, "Wes Anderson's Dream House," *Observer* (June 4, 2001).

p. 175 "Boutiquing" of Harlem: Sharon Zukin, "New Retail Capital and Neighborhood Change: Boutiques and Gentrification in New York City," *City & Community* 8, no. 1 (March 2009): 47–64; and Bruce D. Haynes, "In Terms of Harlem," in *The Ghetto: Contemporary Global Issues and Controversies*, ed. Ray Hutchison and Bruce D. Haynes (Westview Press, 2011), 111–35.